MW01627505

Second edition

Copyright © 2005, 2007 The LFL Group, LLC

All rights reserved. No portion of this book may be reproduced, stored in a retrieval system, or transmitted in any form or by any means—electronic, mechanical, photocopy, recording or any other—except for brief quotations in printed reviews, without the prior permission of the publisher.

The *Steps to Freedom in Christ* section of this book, by Neil T. Anderson. Copyright © 2005 All rights reserved. No portion of this section may be reproduced, stored in a retrieval system, or transmitted in any form or by any means—electronic, mechanical, photocopy, recording or any other—except for brief quotations in printed reviews, without prior permission from Neil T. Anderson.

All Scripture quotations, unless otherwise indicated, are taken from the Holy Bible, New International Version (NIV). Copyright 1973, 1978, 1984 by International Bible Society. Used by permission of Zondervan Publishing House. All Rights Reserved.

LFL

Published by The LFL Group, P.O. Box 605, Long Lake, Minnesota 55356

Design by Andrew Manthei
www.MantheiDesign.com
Printed in the United States of America.

ISBN 978-0-9719958-6-4

Foreword from Jamie

It is important to make clear that in its original form, this book was written for Christian men only. It came at what seems to have been a perfect time. There were enough God-fearing men who were tired of relying upon their own self-discipline to save them from lust that they were ready to run after a spiritual perspective like this in faith. What has been the result? Several things, but the greatest is that it has truly set men free. The book hasn't set men free. Lowell Seashore, the author of the book and their mentor, hasn't set them free. A set of principles throughout the book hasn't set them free. **Jesus has set them free.**

Another amazing thing that has begun to happen through God's truths written about in this book is it has changed so many men's lives that women are being strongly affected.

Yet those of us who have men in our lives who have experienced sexual freedom from the ministry of LFL have begun to discover we too have much to learn about and pursue in the way of freedom in Christ. Much of it lies well kept and covered in our own sexual bondages and misconceptions. So, after several years of intense impact on men, what better way to watch new fruit grow between men and women sexually than to bring light to these same truths for women?

In essence the truths are the same, so there aren't many differences between the men's and women's version of this book. There are fine details that are different, as God created us much the same, yet much different from one another. However, when we look at this from a spiritual perspective and from the perspective of Satan attacking a most beautiful part of who we are, the battle is much the same, and both men and women need to learn how to fight and win that battle.

God is far greater than our little minds can conceive. He has much truth to expose to us and a ton of beauty to uncover as we run wild in the freedom He has for us. So let's allow Jesus to uncover some lies and breathe life into death, and let's ask ourselves some big questions. Let's discover what accountability truly looks like for us outside of a "self-controlled" and shame-based system and lavish in the wonder of our sexuality as women. He has done a mighty work in His creation of both men and women. Until we experience the freedom He offers us, we will only know in part how great sex and our sexuality were meant to be.

I ask you to read this book for no other reason than because you are ready to be transformed by JESUS. This material is simple, but it is God's truth for us wrapped in grace, authority, boldness and simplicity all at the same time. No one chapter fully makes sense without all the others, so chew on it all. And while you do, I pray that you will dance with excitement as you begin the journey to living fully in who God created you to be.

Enjoy Him, Beautiful!

Jamie Book

Foreword from Lowell

Unveil: Beginning the Process of Lust Free Living is our attempt to give you principles from the Bible as they apply to sexual lusts. They can and should be applied to all areas of your life. I pray Jesus will lead you into His freedom using *Unveil* as a way to speak God's truth into your life.

I originally wrote Lust Free Living (LFL) as a Bible study for young men in my church. I know sexuality is a wonderful and powerful gift from God to us, and the evil one was using it against us very effectively. LFL is my attempt to give you tools to make your sexuality what God intended it to be in your life—wonderful, exciting and pure.

I am very excited to now offer it to women also and hope you learn to fully enjoy your freedom in Christ which comes from knowing who you really are in His eyes. The absolute realization that you have value and are loved just as you are. Your worth and value does not come from your sexuality, your body, what you do for work, how you perform, how much money you have or your relationship with men. Your worth comes from your Creator and what he says about you. Your sexuality is a wonderful gift.

My prayer is that you learn how to actually take thoughts captive in obedience to Christ. That you can learn how to renew your mind daily with the Holy Spirit, renounce lies and deceptions and accept truth. In other words, learn how to, in a practical way, fight spiritually first.

My thanks to Jamie Book who has done an artful job of writing the sexuality parts of this workbook from a woman's perspective. I am sure you will all find them thought-provoking and enlightening. The rest of the book is basically the same as the men's book, *Dangerous Men: Beginning the Process of Lust Free Living.*

And my sincere thanks goes to my loving, kind and always supportive wife, Susie. She is the most wonderful woman I have ever met and is more of a reflection of Jesus in her service to others than anyone I know. She gives to others in more ways than I can even dream of. Without her I couldn't do the ministry God has called us to do. She is the love of my life, and I dedicate this book to her.

Fighting together for the Kingdom,

Lowell

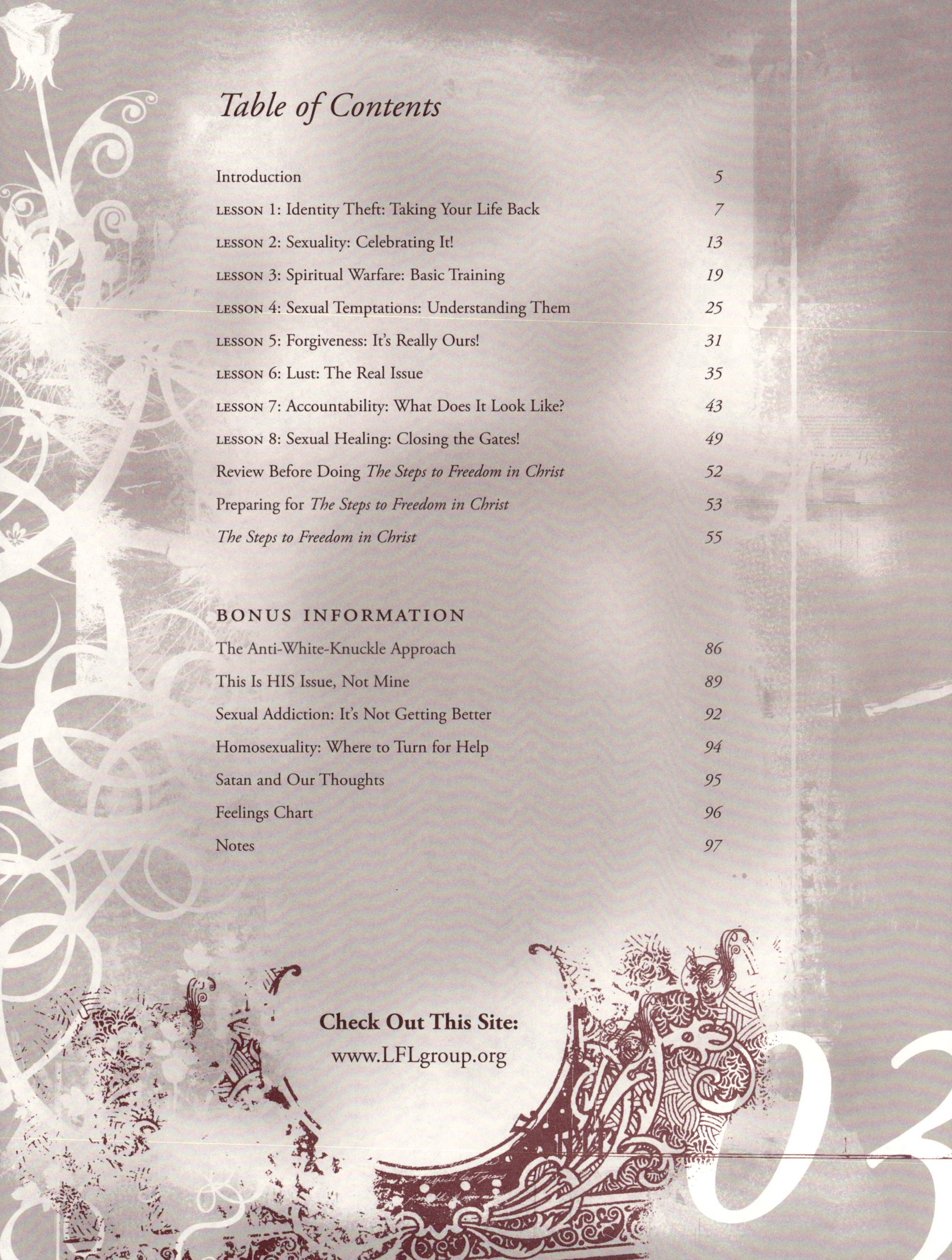

Table of Contents

BONUS INFORMATION

Check Out This Site:

www.LFLgroup.org

Introduction

Women,

Do you sometimes feel alone in your secret thoughts and actions?

Do you feel like you are the only female who struggles with the things you do?

Do you think you will never get over the shame of your negative sexual choices?

Are your life, your relationship with Christ, your relationships with others, your joy and your peace being disrupted by negative choices you make regarding sexual issues?

Are you trying to fight these battles on your own and losing?

If you answer "yes" or even "sometimes" to any of these questions, then you will want to read on. You will learn how to live free—lust free!

Advisory Notice

The thief comes only to steal and kill and destroy; I have come that they may have life, and have it to the full (John 10:10).

Now the evil one, seeing that sex is such a wonderful gift to us from God, decided to try and steal it away. To do this, he devised a great scheme to elaborately twist our thinking and cause us to use God's great gift of sex in unhealthy and harmful ways.

Almost all of Satan's temptations are to keep us from trusting God, because he wants us to believe that Jesus is not enough, that we really need something or someone else to fulfill us. It could be with giving away sex for love, uncontrolled masturbation, loneliness, lustful fantasies, being sexually active outside of God's boundaries or a variety of other things. Satan wants to harm us by using our sexuality to create bondages in our lives.

When we buy into Satan's deceptions, following our old sinful nature, we rebel against God's plan. God's plan is for us to be free from all bondage and to enjoy being sexual. If God created sex for us to enjoy and created our sexuality, then why don't we trust His plan in this area? All we have to do is obey Him and choose His plan, and we can enjoy being a sexual person. Married or single, it makes no difference. Isn't that just like our God!

The following lessons will teach us what lust looks like for women and how to live free from it.

1. Identity Theft: Taking Your Life Back
This first lesson shows us how to renew our minds as to who we really are.

2. Sexuality: Celebrating It!
This lesson helps us uncover the lies that we might believe when it comes to sex and sexuality. It is a fresh look at how God sees our sexuality.

3. Spiritual Warfare: Basic Training
As Christians we must get it through our heads that we are to fight in the spiritual realm first, and then deal with the emotional, mental and physical areas. This lesson will help us learn how.

4. Sexual Temptations: Understanding Them
It is important to understand how to think about and know what to do with sexual temptations.

5. Forgiveness: It's Really Ours!
This lesson gives us a better understanding about forgiveness as it relates to sexual issues.

6. Lust: The Real Issue
We need to learn to focus on the problem and not the symptoms.

7. Accountability: What Does It Look Like?
This lesson explains why we should be accountable and what that looks like. Health is found in interdependence, not independence.

8. Sexual Healing: Closing the Gates!
We all desperately need healing from our sexual sins. This lesson helps us discover how.

The Steps to Freedom in Christ
Neil T. Anderson's spiritual and moral inventory is a great weapon in our spiritual battle.

Bonus Information

The Anti-White-Knuckle Approach
This Is HIS Issue, Not Mine
Jamie Book shares an intimate view into how she and her husband fight against lust.
Sexual Addiction: It's Not Getting Better
If you have followed all the steps in this book and still struggle a lot, check this information out.
Homosexuality: Where to Turn for Help
Two organizations and an excellent CD that will help you understand and deal with this issue. Check out this extra information to assist you in the process.
Satan and Our Thoughts
Feelings Chart

Please read these lessons in order. They build on each other for understanding.

LESSON 1

Identity Theft: Taking Your Life Back

And that's the way it was with us before Christ came. We were slaves to the spiritual powers of this world. But when the right time came, God sent his Son, born of a woman, subject to the law. God sent him to buy freedom for us who were slaves of the law, so that he could adopt us as his very own children. And because you Gentiles have become his children, God has sent the Spirit of his Son into your hearts, and now you can call God your dear Father. Now you are no longer a slave but God's own child. And since you are his child, everything he has belongs to you. (Galatians 4:3–7 NLT)

Yet to all who received him, to those who believed in his name, he gave the right to become children of God. (John 1:12)

Concept

"Understanding your identity in Christ is absolutely essential for your success at living a victorious Christian life. No person can consistently behave in a way that's inconsistent with the way he perceives himself."[i] Dr. Neil T. Anderson

Who we are and how we see ourselves determines how we act and live, so this question of identity is of extreme importance to us. Often this seems to be the missing chapter in our thinking.

In this chapter I will give you an outline view of the concepts, but I think you should do more reading on the subject later. One of the best books and teaching on this subject is *Victory Over Darkness* by Dr. Neil T. Anderson. I highly recommend you read it. I also recommend Donald Miller's book *Searching for God Knows What.*

Fighting

Read the following statements from a bookmark from Freedom In Christ Ministries. See if you can tell which statements are God's truth and which ones are lies from the evil one. Where do you really get your identity from?

You are a sinner because you sin.
You are a saint (one declared righteous by God) who sins.

Your identity comes from what you have done.
Your identity comes from what God has done for you.

Your identity comes from what people say about you.
Your identity comes from what God says about you.

Your behavior tells you what to believe about yourself.
Your belief about yourself determines your behavior.[ii]

Yes, the first lines are all lies. But the sad fact is that most of us believe or at least live by them. When we gave our lives to Jesus and started following Him there wasn't a "reset" button that we could push to make all our old habits (or what the Bible calls our flesh) go away. **We have to learn how to renew our minds**.

Do not conform any longer to the pattern of this world, but be transformed by the renewing of your mind. Then you will be able to test and approve what God's will is—his good, pleasing and perfect will (Romans 12:2).

We have to choose to believe the promises of God about us. We have to get God's truth into our minds. Not only do we need to think as we should about who we are, we must also let these truths filter into our hearts (easier said than done).

God's Girl

Sometimes familiarity is a problem with those of us who have grown up in the Christian church. We hear about a concept or truth so many times that it fails to become a reality to us.

The reality is that we really are God's children, adopted into His family. Our identity in Jesus Christ is one of the most basic principles in the Bible. We seem to intellectually know it, but it does not permeate our lives like it should. We need our hearts to soak in this truth.

Here is the truth (read these out loud):

His unchanging plan has always been to adopt us into his own family by bringing us to himself through Jesus Christ. And this gave him great pleasure (Ephesians 1:5 New Living Translation NLT).

I love that last part *"...this gave him great pleasure."*

But to all who believed him and accepted him, he gave the right to become children of God. They are reborn! This is not a physical birth resulting from human passion or plan—this rebirth comes from God (John 1:12–13 NLT).

But the person who is joined to the Lord is one spirit with him (1 Corinthians 6:17 NLT).

It is difficult to sink this truth into our hearts. We have all heard it said that we are a child of God, but somehow we still don't get it. Identity is a concept that we have to get from the head to the heart in order to live it out every day. If we change one word it can become new to us. It can start to mean something again. Let's change the word "children" to "girl." Say it out loud, We are God's girls, I am God's girl. I am His daughter, adopted into His family, He is my daddy, and I am His girl. No matter our age, we are our daddy's little girl. Now doesn't that somehow resonate with all of us? What girl hasn't at one time wanted to associate herself as her daddy's little girl? Even if our relationship with our earthly father didn't fit this idea, if we are honest, we all have that desire somewhere in us. And this is just what we are to our Father and our Creator—HIS GIRL!

I heard a saying once and I adapted it to this: ***Be a woman to women, a warrior to demons, and always a child of God.*** You are God's girl! He is your Father!

The more you say that out loud, the more it becomes believable for you. However, it is not true because you say it to yourself many times; it is true because the Bible says it is true, and you make the choice to believe the truth. It is also spoken to your heart by the Holy Spirit, and it becomes real in your soul.

We often seem to go to lesser gods to satisfy our wants, needs and desires. Somehow they never satisfy our deep longings. We turn to rebellion, cynicism, alcohol, lust and other gods for comfort. We have trouble learning how to go to the true Comforter as our only source of comfort.

Jesus talks to us about how to abide in His love. *I am the vine; you are the branches. Those who remain in me, and I in them, will produce much fruit. For apart from me you can do nothing. Anyone who does not remain in me is thrown away like a useless branch and withers. Such branches are gathered into a pile to be burned. But if you remain in me and my words remain in you, you may ask for anything you want, and it will be granted! When you produce much fruit, you are my true disciples. This brings great glory to my Father. I have loved you even as the Father has loved me. Remain in my love* (John 15:5–9 NLT).

We seem to wander from His love so easily and without much of a fight. Hopefully as you go through the rest of this study you will learn how to fight and how to remain in your true identity. You are truly God's girl! Satan is always opposed to God's truth and will always try to trick us into thinking and believing that we are unacceptable, unworthy and will never be seen by God as important. We need to abide in who we are in Christ; abide in Him, who is in us.

Another amazing thought comes from the story Jesus told about the lost sons. Two sons, equally lost, one usually called the prodigal son and the other known as the good son. The father in the story represents God Himself. Here is the story taken from Luke 15 NLT.

To illustrate the point further, Jesus told them this story:
"A man had two sons. The younger son told his father, 'I want my share of your estate now, instead of waiting until you die.' So his father agreed to divide his wealth between his sons.

"A few days later this younger son packed all his belongings and took a trip to a distant land, and there he wasted all his money on wild living. About the time his money ran out, a great famine swept over the land, and he began to starve. He persuaded a local farmer to hire him to feed his pigs. The boy became so hungry that even the pods he was feeding the pigs looked good to him. But no one gave him anything.

"When he finally came to his senses, he said to himself, 'At home even the hired men have food enough to spare, and here I am, dying of hunger! I will go home to my father and say, "Father, I have sinned against both heaven and you, and I am no longer worthy of being called your son. Please take me on as a hired man."' (Notice the son coming back to the father also didn't understand how God forgives.)

"So he returned home to his father. And while he was still a long distance away, his father saw him coming. Filled with love and compassion, he ran to his son, embraced him, and kissed him. His son said to him, 'Father, I have sinned against both heaven and you, and I am no longer worthy of being called your son.'

"But his father said to the servants, 'Quick! Bring the finest robe in the house and put it on him. Get a ring for his finger, and sandals for his feet. And kill the calf we have been fattening in the pen. We must celebrate with a feast, for this son of mine was dead and has now returned to life. He was lost, but now he is found.' So the party began."

What the father does here is quite amazing. He puts a robe, a ring and footwear on his boy. Then he throws a party. The robe, ring and footwear all symbolize that he accepts his boy back as part of the royal family—not a servant, but his son. It is equally true for God's daughters, His girls! God, our Father, does not listen to our lame attempts to make things right, because He knows they are worthless. Instead, He fully restores us and welcomes us back with open arms!

Important Stuff

Freedom In Christ Ministries (FICM.org) has prepared the following list of verses about God's truth and put them in many different formats and places. Read these verses out loud to yourself every day for at least two weeks. Reprogram, relearn, retrain and renew your mind with these truths. Read them in your spare time, tape them to your bathroom mirror and read them out loud each morning, post them on your bed. Do any creative thing you want, but start believing in who God says you are. Know and accept who we truly are IN CHRIST.

I am accepted...

I am God's child. John 1:12
I am Christ's friend. John 15:15
I have been justified. Romans 5:1
I am united with the Lord, and I am one in spirit with Him. 1 Corinthians 6:17

I have been bought with a price. I belong to God. 1 Corinthians 6:19–20
I am a member of Christ's body. 1 Corinthians 12:27
I am a saint. Ephesians 1:1
I have been adopted as God's child. Ephesians 1:5
I have direct access to God through the Holy Spirit. Ephesians 2:18
I have been redeemed and forgiven of all my sins. Colossians 1:14
I am complete in Christ. Colossians 2:10

I am secure.
I am free forever from condemnation. Romans 8:1–2
I am assured that all things work together for good. Romans 8:28
I am free from any condemning charges against me. Romans 8:31–34
I cannot be separated from the love of God. Romans 8:35–39
I have been established, anointed and sealed by God. 2 Corinthians 1:21–22
I am hidden with Christ in God. Colossians 3:3
I am confident that the good work God has begun in me will be perfected. Philippians 1:6
I am a citizen of heaven. Philippians 3:20
I have not been given a spirit of fear, but of power, love and a sound mind. 2 Timothy 1:7
I can find grace and mercy in time of need. Hebrews 4:15–16
I am born of God, and the evil one cannot touch me. 1 John 5:18

I am significant.
I am the salt and light of the earth. Matthew 5:13–14
I am a branch of the true vine, a channel of His life. John 15:1,5
I have been chosen and appointed to bear fruit. John 15:16
I am a personal witness of Christ. Acts 1:8
I am God's temple. 1 Corinthians 3:16
I am a minister of reconciliation for God. 2 Corinthians 5:17–21
I am God's co-worker. 2 Corinthians 6:1
I am seated with Christ in the heavenly realm. Ephesians 2:6
I am God's workmanship. Ephesians 2:10
I may approach God with freedom and confidence. Ephesians 3:12
I can do all things through Christ who strengthens me. Philippians 4:13

Hmmm?

"The essence of all temptation is the invitation to live independent of God and fulfill legitimate needs in the world, the flesh or the devil instead of in Christ."[iii] Dr. Neil T. Anderson

For me, the bottom line always seems to be the enemy tempting me with the thought that Jesus is not enough. He is not enough to meet my needs. He is not enough to take care of me the way I should be. He is not enough to deal with my fears. He is just not big enough—an absolute lie of the devil! **Jesus is always enough for me.**

Say this out loud: "In your name, Jesus, I reject the lie that you are not enough for me, and you won't take care of me. I accept the truth that you are enough, you have paid the price for my sins and you love me."

We do not often hear from this world that we are secure, accepted or significant. I began the LFL study in a deep struggle with my identity. I knew that God thought more of me than I thought of myself, but as far as what that was, I was at a loss. My entire life I had thought of myself as nothing more or less than what the world thought of me. If I got an A on a test I was smart. If I had a boyfriend I was pretty. If I went to Bible study I was a "good Christian." God used the LFL study to show me that not only was my thinking misguided, it was altogether wrong. I am an intelligent, beautiful, SAINT not because of what I have done but because of who Jesus is and what he has done for me!

Those words--secure, accepted and significant--describe desires that reside deep in my heart. I realized that I had spent a great deal of my life striving for those three things, and I had found them and did not even know it. After learning more about my identity through this chapter, I spent some time going through the verses described and reading them in context in my Bible. The Scripture really came alive to me during that time. My view of myself changed to look a little more like Christ's view, and it was freeing.

I also discovered that my identity struggle is not something I can learn about and check off on my "to do" list as being completed. I have to surrender my misguided view of myself to the Lord every day. I review His word and reprogram my thoughts to be more like His all the time. I have discovered the more I do this the more freedom I experience to be the woman God made me to be to love myself and love others more completely.

NiKKi

Sexuality: Celebrating It!

So God created human beings[a] in his own image. In the image of God he created them; male and female he created them. (Genesis 1:27 NLT)

Concept

Celebrate our sexuality? How in the world do you do that and remain pure before God and pure in relationships?

For many of us, we have grown up not clearly understanding our sexuality and God's intentions for it. Maybe we tried to stuff, stifle or ignore it because we thought it was a negative thing. That could not be more false. In order to celebrate this amazing part of who God created us to be, we must first uncover some lies so we can clearly see the truth given to us in God's word.

What is true?

- We are created in God's image.
- God created sex.
- God created us sexual people.
- God created us male and female.
- God wants us to have **great** sex (after all He invented it).
- God intended sexual intercourse to be one of the greatest expressions of marital intimacy.

Of course, Satan will try to mess up something that is this positive and good for humans. Satan twists our sexuality from something wonderful, as God intended it to be, into something shameful, lustful, strictly physical and/or something to control or to use as a source of power. WE NEED TO RETHINK HOW WE THINK ABOUT OUR SEXUALITY.

We are sexual. We have physical desires. Our bodies were made by God to do certain things to produce stimulation and to respond physically in ways that are amazing. We need to celebrate and enjoy that. Our mind, our emotions and our spirit were all created to desire certain things sexually and to respond in a way that is very natural and positive. With this in mind, the question that follows is often, "Then what are we to do with this part of us?" The answer is simple: ENJOY BEING SEXUAL! CELEBRATE IT! That doesn't mean take advantage of it, tempt with it, manipulate it or enhance it. JUST ENJOY BEING A SEXUAL PERSON. This might not make sense to many of us at first, so let's look at it through a different example:

Most of us love to eat. We have this craving and desire for food. We eat to nourish our bodies. So let's say we have just had a meal and our stomach is satisfied. We go for a walk and pass a bakery that has been baking fresh goods all day. The aroma is amazing and our mouths are watering even though we aren't hungry. It is so cool that our bodies respond in this way. It is so natural and good. Part of why God created us to respond this way is so we might enjoy nourishing our body when it is time to eat. We should celebrate and enjoy the way our intricate bodies work in times like this. That doesn't mean we should bolt into the bakery and indulge in everything they have to offer us. A healthy response would be to pause and notice how our body is responding to our senses, celebrate how cool it is and move on.

So ENJOY and CELEBRATE your sexuality! Be aware of all that it is, how it all works and how enjoyable that part of you is. It is natural, good and God-given.

Here is the hard part: Our surroundings (the world) mess with our minds from the time we are little. We are told the beautiful, erotic and sexual parts of us are something to use for power and self-fulfillment. We receive the message we are no longer simply beautiful just as we are, but we are to become a "temptress" to draw the attention of men. Then as Christians we are taught we are to live pure and "save ourselves" until we are married. Most people have interpreted that to mean we are to stuff or hide the sexual aspects of who we are and not recognize them until we are married. When those two worlds collide there is confusion, shame, fear, self-destruction, manipulation, etc. It is hard to understand God made us sexual—married or unmarried, man or woman—and He wants us to celebrate that part of us.

Funny how the enemy switches sides so quickly. One minute he's whispering in our ear, "It's okay to fantasize about that guy. It's not going to hurt anything." So we go ahead and indulge in lustful thinking. Then the enemy shows up again, but this time he's shooting accusations at us, "You really screwed up. You are so stupid--you did it again! See, I knew you weren't good enough to be a Christian." Lies, lies and more lies, always accusing us: One of Satan's greatest desires is to keep us away from God and the enjoyment and freedom that come from living within God's boundaries for us.

Along with enjoying how we were created, God also wants us to be free. In fact this is the key to truly enjoying our sexuality. He wants us to be:

- Free from all the stereotypes the world puts on us as to what is beautiful and sexy.
- Free from the desperate need for acceptance from a man.
- Free from the desire to gain power and control by using our bodies to manipulate men (that "temptress" role).
- Free from any addictions we have.
- Free from lust.
- Free from romance novels, women's magazines, TV shows and Internet sites that keep us thinking lustfully.
- Free from pornography and pornographic stories.
- Free from being a slave in any way to masturbation.
- Free from the game of comparison with other women.
- Free from our old sinful nature with all its sexual lusts.

He wants us to stop living in the bondage of the standards of this world, of our twisted interpretations of purity, of our painful experiences, and break free so we can celebrate, love and serve! It is in purity that we will experience the fullness of all that God intended our sexuality to be. *It is for freedom that Christ has set us free. Stand firm, then and do not let yourselves be burdened again by a yoke of slavery* (Galatians 5:1).

God also wants us to enjoy Him, the one who made us this way. We don't want to get tricked into worshiping the thing that He created (sex). We need to enjoy worshiping the Creator Himself. After all, He is pretty creative!

Fighting

When it comes to celebrating our sexuality, it must be a healthy, pure thing. In order for that to be the case we need to have boundaries. But here's the deal—we need to rethink how we think of boundaries, so check this out:

As Christian women, we can get caught up in playing a game of rules of DOs and DON'Ts. Rules like don't wear this; do wear that; don't go here; do go there; don't look at a guy like __________; don't be alone with a guy at night; don't go this far; you can go *this* far; etc. The list could go on, but you get the point. When it comes to our purity and the purity of the guys around us, we have this set of rules in our head. Some people follow their rules better than others, but the point is that **we are trying in our <u>own</u> strength and power to control things**.

What ends up happening is we are still sexual, but we don't see the beauty of it. Instead we see it only as something to control. We are confused by what to do with our desires. So we try to maintain most of these rules, but somehow still be that "temptress."

A lot of times we have all of these rules set up because we are afraid, and if we put all these things around us, then we think we will have nothing to fear. Maybe we are afraid of ourselves, or we are afraid of men. Or maybe our faith in the power and self-control we have in Christ Jesus isn't established; therefore we fear that God in fact isn't enough and that He *doesn't* strengthen us. The truth is, *"I can do everything through Him who gives me strength"* (Philippians 4:13).

First of all God tells us hundreds of times in His word to "fear not." So if our rules are based in fear, and fear is not from God, then it can be assumed that we will struggle to maintain those rules because their foundation is shaky. But if we truly embrace the truths that God gave us, to keep the marriage bed pure (Hebrews 13:4) and to love our neighbor as ourselves (Romans 13:9–10), then we will learn how to fight spiritually first against temptation, impurity and lustful thoughts. After that God will lead us to healthy boundaries. Boundaries and rules are crucial! They become effective when they are established out of freedom, understanding, celebration and excitement, rather than legalism, fear, ignorance or pride.

The rules are few. The main rule is to do everything in love—God's love. Not just our own love, but the same UNSELFISH and UNCONDITIONAL love that Christ showed toward us. I once heard Miles McPherson talk about sex and he said, **"Love desires to please someone else at the expense of self because love wants to *give.* Lust wants to please self at the expense of someone else because lust wants to *get.*"**[iv] When we choose to live outside God's boundaries, we are not choosing love. I think that is a good way of thinking about it. Memorize it!

Important Stuff

"To define sexuality in mere physical terms misses the most important dimension of human sexuality—the spiritual. Sexuality is not just something that joins our bodies; it also involves the joining of our spirits. (Meeting) our physical needs... is not all we want. We also want spiritual union. We want 'belonging.' We want to be the object of someone's interest and care. We want reciprocal faithfulness and trust, and we want the assurance and peace that those bring. Any definition of sexuality that excludes those things is inadequate. Sexuality should be defined, therefore, as the human potential for the complete sharing of our whole selves, both body and spirit with a person of the other sex. Because our sexuality links the spiritual to the physical, no amount of mere physical activity can create the wholeness for which our hearts long."[v] Thomas F. Jones, Associate Director of Fresh Start Seminars.

As emotional, erotic and beautiful women in this world, we sometimes get fooled into believing we have to be "temptresses" to meet our sexual desires, have fun and "feel" loved. Those ideas, however, are simply more of Satan's lies. In the next lesson we will learn about how to deal with the enemy's accusations and lies.

When I first saw the title for this chapter, "Sexuality: Celebrating It!," I thought it was a joke (and a cruel one at that). The idea that my sexuality could be celebrated didn't fit at all with what I had seen, been taught and especially felt. In many ways I was angry such a thing could even be suggested, and more than that, I was scared to think it might actually be true. But as I read on, I began to see how I had it all wrong.

I thought my sexuality was to blame. For so long I had punished myself for having sexual desires, never realizing my sexuality was God-given. Desire seemed so untamed, wild and uncontrolled. I thought there was no way it could be from God. I had made my sexuality into such a bad thing that I began to be trapped in a cycle of shame. I realized when I rejected what God had created, I was really rejecting my Creator. This rejection caused me to think that God enjoyed my struggle to be pure. Instead of a loving God, I saw him more as a giant with a stick who was waiting for me to screw up. My whole view of God had been distorted by trying to stifle my sexuality.

Over time God restored to me the truth about His character. I began to see Him as a loving Father, characterized by goodness, mercy and forgiveness--a God always ready to forgive my lust and redeem me from my wounds. I realized it was okay for me to be aroused. My body was created by God to do that! And celebration didn't mean I could let my feelings and desires rule me. It is a balance. And through fighting spiritually God helps me to walk pure before Him.

Libbie

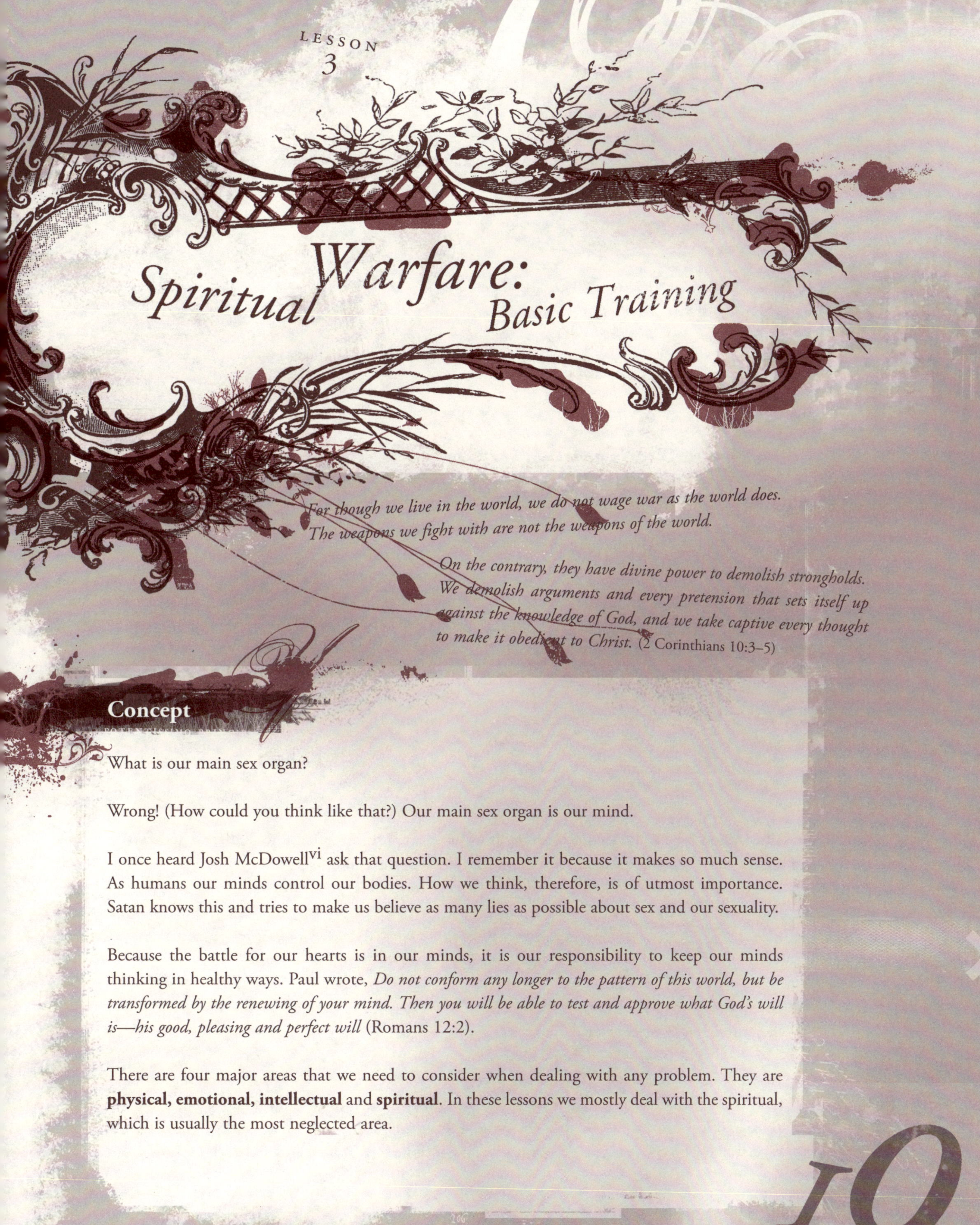

LESSON 3

Spiritual Warfare: Basic Training

For though we live in the world, we do not wage war as the world does. The weapons we fight with are not the weapons of the world.

On the contrary, they have divine power to demolish strongholds. We demolish arguments and every pretension that sets itself up against the knowledge of God, and we take captive every thought to make it obedient to Christ. (2 Corinthians 10:3–5)

Concept

What is our main sex organ?

Wrong! (How could you think like that?) Our main sex organ is our mind.

I once heard Josh McDowell[vi] ask that question. I remember it because it makes so much sense. As humans our minds control our bodies. How we think, therefore, is of utmost importance. Satan knows this and tries to make us believe as many lies as possible about sex and our sexuality.

Because the battle for our hearts is in our minds, it is our responsibility to keep our minds thinking in healthy ways. Paul wrote, *Do not conform any longer to the pattern of this world, but be transformed by the renewing of your mind. Then you will be able to test and approve what God's will is—his good, pleasing and perfect will* (Romans 12:2).

There are four major areas that we need to consider when dealing with any problem. They are **physical, emotional, intellectual** and **spiritual**. In these lessons we mostly deal with the spiritual, which is usually the most neglected area.

We need to learn how to renew our minds by fighting spiritually first when it comes to lust and sexual issues, then the rest of the battle is a lot easier. We still have to deal with our emotions, disciplining our thinking patterns and physical activities. It just doesn't work very well if we try and use only self-control to fight lust, because even people with an extreme amount of self-discipline can only get so close to lust free living without learning to fight spiritually.

Fighting

And there was war in heaven. Michael and his angels fought against the dragon, and the dragon and his angels fought back. But he was not strong enough, and they lost their place in heaven. The great dragon was hurled down—that ancient serpent called the devil, or Satan, who leads the whole world astray. He was hurled to the earth, and his angels with him. Then I heard a loud voice in heaven say:

"Now have come the salvation and the power and the kingdom of our God, and the authority of his Christ. For the accuser of our brothers, who accuses them before our God day and night, has been hurled down. They overcame him by the blood of the Lamb and by the word of their testimony; they did not love their lives so much as to shrink from death. Therefore rejoice you heavens and you who dwell in them! But woe to the earth and the sea, because the devil has gone down to you! He is filled with fury, because he knows that his time is short" (Revelation 12:7–12).

Rev. Ed Silvoso describes the spiritual battle from this verse in a very easy way for us to remember and understand:[vii]

Satan's Weapons	Type of Warfare	Satan's Role	God's Counter Provisions
#1 Sin	Active	tempter	The blood of the Lamb (Jesus' payment for sin)
#2 Accusations	Passive	accuser	Who we are in Christ (Word of their testimony)
#3 Strongholds	Dormant	deceiver	Dying to self (Did not... shrink from death)

Illustration for #1 Sin, Active Warfare: If we entertain lustful thoughts, we know we have sinned right away. We alsoknow that Jesus' death (the blood of the Lamb) paid for our sins when He died on the cross. All we have to do is accept the gift of forgiveness and move on. Here is a prayer for this situation: *"Lord Jesus, I humbly accept the forgiveness that you offer me for my lustful thoughts about __________ (state the lustful thought), and I acknowledge that I do not deserve it, but that you freely offer forgiveness to me. Thank you Lord Jesus, I accept your gift of forgiveness."*

Illustration for #2 Accusations, Passive Warfare: We totally underestimate the destructive power of accusations. Somehow we don't get it!

After we have sinned, and after we have accepted our forgiveness, Satan starts accusing us so we won't believe that the price Jesus paid was enough. He wants us to think that we have to pay a price and feel bad about ourselves for sinning. He wants us to think that God will only forgive us if we beat up on ourselves emotionally and continue to feel shameful and bad. He also wants us to believe we are stupid, awful and worthless. All of Satan's accusations basically come down to this: Jesus is just not enough for you—don't trust Jesus. What lies! The truth is that we are not worthy and never will be worthy of Jesus' forgiveness! It is by God's grace that we can receive this gift of forgiveness. The good news, however, is this: **We already have been forgiven, and all we have to do is accept it.**

According to Rev. Silvoso's chart, how do we fight Satan's accusations? We fight by verbally stating the truth about who we are in Christ (the word of our testimony). To fight the spiritual battle for your mind when Satan accuses, say something like this out loud, *"In the name of Jesus, I renounce the lie that I am a worthless person and need to 'feel bad enough' so that I can be forgiven. I accept the truth that the price Jesus paid was enough. I am His child. I am His friend. I am forgiven whether I feel like it or not. Jesus, help me to always know your truth."*

Illustration for #3 Strongholds, Dormant Warfare: Most sexual struggles qualify as strongholds. Dr. Neil Anderson says, "Strongholds are negative patterns of thought which are burned into our minds either through repetition over time or through one-time traumatic experiences."[viii]

According to Rev. Silvoso, "A spiritual stronghold is a mindset impregnated with hopelessness that causes us to accept as unchangeable situations that we know are contrary to the will of God."[ix] Remember that strongholds are thoughts and concepts located in our minds.

So a stronghold shows up in how we think about things. Here is an example: You know the Bible says, *And God is faithful. He will keep the temptation from becoming so strong you can't stand up against it. When you are tempted, he will show you a way out so you will not give in to it* (1 Corinthians 10:13 NIV). You know it in your head, but you do not really believe it when a temptation comes around. You still think somehow it is too strong to resist and you will just end up giving in anyway... so why not give in now? This is a stronghold because you live like it is true even though you know it to be contrary to the Word of God.

Why don't most Christians understand how the spiritual realm works in our world? Maybe we just get uncomfortable when we read it; maybe we believe lies that Satan is more powerful than he really is. Maybe we don't really believe the verse.

Important Stuff

It is important to understand that Satan sometimes has a **legal right** to **bug** us as Christians. He gains this legal right because of our unconfessed sin or lies that we believe. Sin, left unconfessed and unhealed, can then turn into a stronghold. This is why, when we're fighting the spiritual battle for our minds, we must accept our forgiveness and confess our sins **immediately after sinning.**

For example, if we accept our forgiveness within five minutes of our sin, then Satan only has five minutes to bug us through that "open gate." If we believe Satan's accusations that Jesus won't forgive us, and don't accept our forgiveness for a few days (weeks or months), then Satan has more time to try to deceive us using that "open gate."

We need to accept our forgiveness immediately, even if our emotions don't feel like it. We do this by claiming and verbalizing the truth.

Think of it this way. Suppose you were a Roman soldier during the time of Christ. The enemy kept firing arrows at you all day long, but lucky for you, you were given a shield. You could deflect the arrows with your shield. One day an arrow somehow knocked a hole in your shield. You have the knowledge to fix it on the spot but you just don't feel like it. You go into battle the next day with a hole in your shield.

Our most efficient way of battling Satan is with God's truth. Make it a truth encounter. Battle by continually speaking and praying God's truth in all situations. We know the truth from His Word, the Bible. Study it so you know what it says. Please don't take someone else's word for it--read it for yourself.

You get the point. What sense does it make to fight with a hole in your shield? You would be a lot less likely to get hit if you patch the hole, right? Why would anyone not plug the hole? That's the way it is with us—the hole is an unconfessed sin. We have the knowledge to fix it, so it only makes sense to patch it up immediately with God's forgiveness.

When we are fighting the spiritual battle for control over our minds, it is very important to remember Jesus has already won this war. We are on the winning side! This means that Satan and his demons have no authority over Christians because we are in Christ. One of Satan's best weapons is to deceive us into thinking that he has power and authority over us. He does have power and authority over the world, but not over those in Christ. That is why Jesus said to the believers in John 8:32, *"Then you will know the truth, and the truth will set you free."* Also in Matthew 28:18–20 Jesus says, *"All authority in heaven and on earth has been given to me. Therefore go and make disciples of all nations, baptizing them in the name of the Father and of the Son and of the Holy Spirit, and teaching them to obey everything I have commanded you. And surely I am with you always, to the very end of the age."*

Satan's authority over us only comes from those unconfessed sins and/or lies that we believe. **All** strongholds can be broken and freedom can be gained. The rest of this workbook focuses on identifying and getting rid of spiritual strongholds in the area of sexuality.

If you suspect a spiritual stronghold in your life, go through *The Steps to Freedom in Christ* at the end of this book. This tool is the best way I have seen to get rid of them. The lesson on sexual healing will show you this process in more detail. This is a very important part of lust free living.

You, dear children, are from God and have overcome them, because the one who is in you is greater than the one who is in the world (1 John 4:4).

Growing up, I was the kind of girl people would call a "church kid." My best friends were almost always from my youth group. I loved going to church, and I always tried to live like a Christian, as I knew it. I did my best to follow all the rules and stayed away from what I learned was "bad."

Looking back, I'd say I was a pretty good kid. However, I had absolutely no idea how much power I had through the Holy Spirit until I went through LFL with my roommate in college. Even though I sat through hundreds of sermons and Bible studies, I never once learned how to really deal with sin or temptation. I was totally blind to the constant spiritual battle occurring around and within me. I bet Satan was pretty happy with where I was at. Even though he knew I had a relationship with Jesus, I was powerless when it came to sexual or emotional temptation. I simply had no idea how to fight spiritually, so when Satan would accuse me of lies like "you aren't as pretty or thin or smart as her" or "he would never be attracted to you," I would just believe the lie every time, weakening my self confidence with each lie.

Consequently, when I started dating my boyfriend in college, I gave into plenty of lies and compromised in my physical relationship with him. Over and over, we would cross the physical boundaries we had created, because all we knew how to do was try really hard not to break a rule, and then beg Jesus to forgive us when we failed. Believing Satan's accusations became so exhausting, and I never felt complete freedom. It turns out trying to follow rules without the power Jesus gives us through the Holy Spirit doesn't work very well.

Luckily, after finally agreeing that I actually did struggle with lust and temptation, my roommate and I started to go through the LFL book and be accountable to one another with the temptations we were facing. The chapter on Spiritual Warfare was especially life-changing for me. The concept of using the power that I have through the Holy Spirit to actively fight against Satan's accusation was profound. At first, praying against lies out loud seemed worthless because I didn't believe it would work. But the more I prayed with confidence, the more power I gained to be able to deal with Satan's lies. It was silly for me to fear Satan because I knew since I have the Holy Sprit, the battle was already won. Even now, Satan will tempt me to believe the same lie over and over, but I know with the Holy Spirit I have the power to reject the lie before it turns into a stronghold.

I know experiencing freedom in Christ is a process, not something you feel once and then always have. I still hear Satan's lies daily, but I'm so thankful for the knowledge I now have to actively fight spiritually against them, instead of just believe Satan's accusations over and over again.

Becky

LFL has helped me be honest with my husband about what is going on in my head and in bringing the truth to light. I really struggled with a vivid fantasy life in my head, and I have not been faithful to my husband if lusting after another man counts as unfaithfulness. When I finally brought this out, it was the beginning of getting rid of a lot of junk that I needed to confess and renounce. I now know how to do that and why it's important. LFL has given me the tools to fight the battle of lust, and I use them to fight other battles as well. Lies that I believe are getting a little easier to see. I still need, and always will need, people to help me see the truth, but now I am open to looking for it and working to get rid of lies. Living in the truth is so freeing. Living free has also made sex with my husband so much better!

Kaydi

LESSON 4

Sexual Temptations: Understanding Them

When tempted, no one should say, "God is tempting me." For God cannot be tempted by evil, nor does he tempt anyone; but each one is tempted when, by his own evil desire, he is dragged away and enticed. Then after desire has conceived, it gives birth to sin; and sin, when it is full-grown, gives birth to death. (James 1:13–15)

Concept

When a lustful thought comes into our heads (which for most of us women is often hard to recognize), it is not a sin according to James. It is a temptation; it only becomes a sin when, by our evil desire, we allow it to pull us into dwelling on the lustful thought. When we continue thinking about it, the thought is conceived in our mind and becomes sin.

Before we go on, it is important to make clear what lust looks like in women's lives. This clarity is necessary because lust in a woman's life looks very different than it does in a man's, and it usually goes unnoticed. For many of us, we have often been confused about what lust is or have not even considered that this is an issue for women. **One of the greatest ways the evil one has kept women in bondage to lust is by deceiving us into thinking we simply don't struggle with it.** For many Christian women, when we think about lust we think of what we need to do to protect the men around us from it. First of all, we don't have the ultimate power to do that because their lust is beyond our control. It is a battle that can only be won by men as they fight against it spiritually first. Secondly, we need to recognize the lust in our own lives and deal with it with power and consistency. It is then that we are able to live in purity and serve ourselves and one another out of freedom and celebration. (See "This Is HIS Issue, Not Mine" on page 89 for more about this subject.)

I think one of the easiest and best definitions of lust is the one we already quoted by Miles McPherson, *"Lust wants to please self at the expense of someone else because lust wants to get."* The definition isn't, "Lust is constantly envisioning or looking at naked people and having an uncontrollable urge to fantasize about having sex with them." No, that may be what lust ends up looking like for some, **but the root issue is much deeper.** Another great way to define lust is "a desire (which is a good and natural thing) becomes what we think is a NEED." Youth Specialties put out a book called "Good Sex," and they did a great job of making it clear when a desire becomes unhealthy, gives birth to temptations, and then becomes sin. Follow this description:

Desire is so easily twisted.
I like it becomes **I want it.**
I want it becomes **I need it.**
I need it becomes **you owe it to me.**
Which becomes **never mind, I'll just take it.**[X]

When we look at that in terms of our attitude towards God regarding our desires and the way our flesh works (temptation), it makes things pretty clear. We have these God-given, healthy desires that turn into what we think of as needs that we meet through our own efforts and control.

So, because of how God created us as women, some of our natural and deepest desires are to be BEAUTIFUL, CHOSEN, NEEDED, ADORED, PROTECTED, IRREPLACEABLE and VALUED. When we feel all of those things, we are very stimulated in every way. This is a good thing! But the dilemma is that in our world today it is pretty hard to feel that way in a pure and healthy sense. Part of the reason is because men are incapable of meeting those desires without Christ. Sometimes, even if the men are healthy and serving or loving us through Christ, we struggle to receive what they have to offer us because our expectations and ideas are distorted. Let's look at the distorted "stuff" a bit.

The world has done a great job of distorting beauty to mean "sexiness," so we have no clue that what defines our beauty really has nothing to do with outward appearance (although in our freedom, that beauty will shine all the way through to the outside).

Your beauty should not come from outward adornment, such as braided hair and the wearing of gold jewelry and fine clothes. Instead it should be that of your inner self, the unfading beauty of a gentle and quiet spirit, which is of great worth in God's sight (1 Peter 3:3–4).

We also have believed the lie that if we want our desires to be fulfilled, we have to DO SOMETHING or BE SOMETHING. Because we associate beauty with "sexiness," we make (or are tempted to make) many attempts on a daily basis, consciously and subconsciously, to exude this sex appeal with our bodies. We do this in hope of filling our desire to be chosen. **There are many women who simply feel hopeless because they don't think they fit the standards of "sexy" in our culture. This often leads to self-destructive behaviors in one way or another.** (If you are in a group, discuss how this concept has affected you personally.)

Another thing we do to meet our desire ("need") to be chosen, is feed into men's lust. Sometimes it is in their lustful response to us that we feel CHOSEN, NEEDED, ADORED, etc. And if that's the best we can get, we'll settle for it. I'm sure by now you are following the twisted web. From this perspective, if we are honest with ourselves, probably most of us can say we have lived our lives far beyond the temptation stage and deep into the sin of our thought-life, self-image and lifestyle.

Ultimately, when you put all of this together and look at our sexual temptations as women, we most definitely struggle with physical temptations and lust, but even above that is the temptation to have power and control in order to have our desires met. All of this is sexual sin—LUST. Wow, how crazy is that!? God's creation of us as women to be uniquely sensitive and gentle has been absolutely messed up by the evil one. He has deceived us into thinking that we are to be powerful and controlling in order to get what we desire. This is such a mask to our true heart!

Incidentally, we can be fairly confident that most of these thoughts and thought processes are not even ours, but are pushed into our head by an evil source. It might just be our old habits (the flesh). The source doesn't really matter. The point is we need to **"capture all of these thoughts and turn them over to Jesus."** I know it is hard, because those thoughts are very deep and consuming, but we need to begin to pinpoint them, pull each one out and deal with each one in the light of Christ. *The Steps to Freedom in Christ* is an awesome tool for this!

Fighting

Let's look at the verse in Corinthians again. *For though we live in the world, we do not wage war as the world does. The weapons we fight with are not the weapons of the world. On the contrary, they have divine power to demolish strongholds. We demolish arguments and every pretension that sets itself up against the knowledge of God, and we take captive every thought to make it obedient to Christ* (2 Corinthians 10:3–5).

Where do arguments and pretensions and thoughts take place? In our minds! The battleground is in our minds! Remember to always **fight spiritually first**. Self-discipline, emotional awareness and intellectual understanding all come later. This definitely goes against what is most natural for us, but God wants us to be warriors too. We need to take our thoughts captive and make them obedient to Christ BEFORE we get all caught up in our emotions. A lot of times we can spare ourselves pain when we fight this way first. We quickly discover when a thought is a lie, and it's over before the emotions even begin!

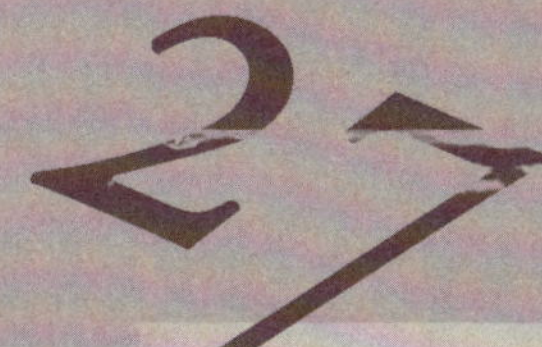

The fighting described above could look like this: When you wake up in the morning and look in the mirror, what is the first thought that comes into your head about your body? Whether it's positive or negative, we need to offer a prayer of praise: *"Dear Heavenly Father, You have created me a beautiful woman. I belong to you, and I thank you and praise you for your creation. I'm holding on to you, Jesus, my Lord and Savior, to help me enjoy my beauty and respond throughout my day with love and not lust."* For most of us, many lies and temptations stem from the thoughts we have when we first glance at ourselves in the morning. Beginning right away, we need to fight spiritually and take captive many thoughts that we have always just bypassed as "normal."

That prayer should also be prayed as you look at a man who you consider beautiful. We too can be tempted and enticed into fantasy, or other sinful responses to our temptations, when we look at a man. Men aren't the *only* visual ones, and **a big need for all of us as women is to offer prayers of praise regarding one another.** Sometimes I think we find each other more fascinating and beautiful than men do. Unfortunately, the sin of lust in our lives greatly affects us in relationship with one another. We would radiate true beauty so much more if we were free to enjoy and celebrate our own beauty and the beauty of every other woman around us. THIS IS A HUGE BATTLE FOR US! Satan has a pretty strong grip on Christian women when it comes to our union, appreciation and love for each other. LUST often plays a very intricate and toxic role in our relationships with each other. (Boldly confess, discuss and pray about this now if you can.)

Remember, Satan cannot read our minds, so he won't obey our thoughts. Only God knows what you're thinking. So say the truth and reject the evil one out loud! Read "Satan and Our Thoughts" in the Bonus Material for more information about Satan putting thoughts in our minds.

It is very important that we learn to immediately recognize when normal enjoyment of our sexuality becomes lustful and sinful. Then we can fight right away, giving no opening for Satan's "legal right" to bug us to try to pull us down with his lies. So let's say a lustful thought comes into your mind. Say out loud (unless you are in a crowded room or something, then say it under your breath), *"No. In Jesus' name I reject this thought because I belong to Jesus, and I choose not to think like that. Get away from me Satan and every enemy of my Lord Jesus Christ."* The exact words are not that important. The three keys here are to RECOGNIZE the thoughts, REJECT the lies and BRING them before Jesus.

It is very important to take captive each thought as soon as it hits our minds. Here are some examples from my life: I stand in my closet and think, "I look pretty good today, my body is up to par, my hair looks good, so I can wear that certain outfit. It will get me the attention I want." Or I used to see a guy and think, "He is good looking. I wonder what it would be like to kiss him." Or I see another woman and think, "She is so pretty. Why can't I have _________ like her?" If I don't take thoughts like that captive, later that day the thought from earlier will be dragging me away and enticing me before I even know it. A lot of times at this point, I'm not even consciously aware of the original thought. I usually don't become aware of it until after I have already given into the temptation.

This is why we need to take our thoughts captive as soon as they come into our minds. For a lot of us, it is hard to even know when these thoughts first come, so it will be good for you to practice openly discussing your thoughts and struggles with other women. As you confess and bring them out into the light, you will become more aware of the thoughts the moment they come, and you can begin to practice taking them captive.

Important Stuff

Most of the Christian writings I have read on the subject of sexual purity focused on what I call a defensive strategy. What I consider a defensive strategy is teaching people to look away when they see someone or something that might make them have lustful thoughts. There are defensive moves that all of us can make that I think are a must—basic fighting—such as a filter on our internet service or getting away from situations where we might be tempted too much. I think every battle plan must have a defense, or we will not win the fight. **But if that is all we have then we are in big trouble.** We cannot and will not win without a good offense.

Our offensive plan laid out in LFL is to learn to fight **SPIRITUALLY FIRST.** Our offense is to fight with the truth of the Word of God, to renounce lies, accept truth and take every thought captive to Jesus—drawing our swords and fighting in the spiritual realm.

We need a great offense and defense. Both are needed; don't be fooled into thinking that obeying the defensive plan alone will win this battle. Attack the lies of the enemy with the power of Jesus, and when the counter attack comes, then you can use some defensive strategies as well.

Unveil: True Stories

Something I did frequently before falling asleep was role-playing in my mind the events and particularly the conversations of my day. As a young woman who rarely dated and didn't have many close guy friends, I desired so badly to be close to a guy. My desire to develop a healthy relationship with a guy and someday get married was a good, God-given desire. The problem was I enjoyed turning that healthy desire into a romantic fantasy, whether it was my current crush or some unnamed hero who had heard of my beauty from far off lands... you get the point.

The thoughts would begin by replaying either a real or imaginary conversation, then they would lead to him kissing me, touching me, and often making love to me. I would be sexually stimulated from my thoughts and often end up masturbating, falling asleep feeling very guilty and confused, and swearing I'd never do it again. You know how that goes. I finally told a dear friend about my struggles and began learning how to fight spiritually. There was so much freedom from the guilt and shame! I no longer felt trapped by my lustful thoughts. In a journal I began praying for my unknown future husband. This was a great channel for me to express my healthy desires to the Lord of having a husband (and even making love!) before they could ever self-implode and become lustful. God blessed me with an amazing man, and I was able to give him that journal full of all my prayers for him on the eve of our wedding.

Katy

When I was dating I would be tempted to depend on my boyfriend to meet my needs. I thought that physical intimacy equaled love and security. Well, I definitely realized the hard way that this wasn't true. In fact, when I used physical intimacy to get love and security it only made me more insecure.

When dealing with temptations, it was also helpful for me to understand that temptations begin as lies. Just like ANY thought, I can call it into God's order by taking it captive to Christ. God will then help me discern which thoughts are temptations. With this in mind, I have realized that I have not sinned when a thought comes into my mind. I do not have to feel like I have lost the battle before the battle has even begun!

The concepts in this chapter have helped me identify and deal with non-sexual temptations. The temptations I am faced with today have to do with shame and cynicism. When I give in to these temptations I shut off hurt feelings, place blame on others, displace anxiety or frustration on others and believe I am not valuable. I know that these actions and thoughts are lies, or the result of a lie, and I do not need to be tied to them. However, I sometimes do not take them captive because I think I can or should be able to deal with them on my own.

It's not until I step outside my comfort zone, take thoughts captive and trust God that I realize I am able to receive His love. Then I can truly love myself and others without any ulterior motives. When my motives are pure I am more honest with myself and more effective when practicing self-control with regard to physical and emotional boundaries in relationships.

Beth

Forgiveness: It's Really Ours!

For as high as the heavens are above the earth, so great is his love for those who fear him; as far as the east is from the west, so far has he removed our transgressions from us. As a father has compassion on his children, so the Lord has compassion on those who fear him; for he knows how we are formed, he remembers that we are dust. (Psalm 103:11–14)

Concept

By dying on the cross, Jesus has already paid the price for our forgiveness and offers it to us for free. We don't have to **ask** for forgiveness, and there is nothing we can do to make us deserving of it. It's a gift that we accept.

Fighting

Question: When did Jesus forgive our sins? Answer: When He died on the cross. You see, all our sins were future to Him, and yet He paid the price for our screw-ups then, almost 2,000 years ago. His work of forgiveness is already complete for the sins of last night and tonight. This is called **grace**—giving us something we don't deserve. We don't now, and never will, deserve to be forgiven. But He loves us so much He offers forgiveness to us as a free gift we just need to accept.

King David writes in Psalm 32:1–2, *Blessed is he whose transgressions are forgiven, whose sins are covered. Blessed is the man whose sin the Lord does not count against him and in whose spirit is no deceit.* Also in Jeremiah 31:34 God says to the people of Israel, *"For I will forgive their wickedness and will remember their sins no more."*

Forgiveness: It's Really Ours!

Here's another cool thing about God. He not only forgives us when we don't deserve it, but He goes another step and forgets about it. No hard feelings, no "get you later" attitudes. He **chooses** to forget it forever. So, if we break down and sin again, afterwards we go to Jesus to accept forgiveness by saying, **"Dear Jesus, I messed up... again. I need to accept your gracious forgiveness." He cuts us off and asks, "What do you mean again? Isn't this the first time?"** Let it sink in a minute—isn't that cool! He chooses to **forgive** and **forget**. What an awesome God!

Repentance

Because Jesus has already forgiven us for our sins of tonight, all we have to do is bring them before Him in repentance. Repentance is our conscious decision to turn away from evil (or disobedience or sin) and turn back to God. After this is done, we stand before God looking just as if we had never sinned (this is what it means to be justified). Sharing, confessing and praying with each other completes the healing in our souls and within the body of Christ (James 5:16).

Even habitual sins are not remembered by Jesus once we accept His forgiveness. We remember our sins, but God chooses to forget them. Because Satan hates God's grace, he tries to use our memories to accuse us with shame: "You are bad; you should feel bad, and Jesus won't forgive you this time. This time is once too many. This time Jesus is ticked off at you. He is no longer in the mood to forgive." **Lies! Lies! And more lies!** Don't believe them! Jesus already forgave us—it's a done deal. All we have to do is to accept the gift and not let Satan deceive us into thinking that Jesus' forgiveness is not enough or not for us. It is for us! The ravaging love of God is a gift to us.

"The saved sinner is prostrate in adoration, lost in wonder and praise. He knows repentance is not what we do in order to earn forgiveness; it is what we do because we have been forgiven. It serves as an expression of gratitude rather than an effort to earn forgiveness. Thus the sequence of forgiveness and then repentance, rather than repentance and then forgiveness, is crucial for understanding the gospel of grace."[xi] Brennan Manning

Shame vs. Guilt: Guilt is a Wonderful Thing

I talked to Keith Hankinson, a friend and great therapist, about the differences between guilt and shame. These are the thoughts that came from our conversation:

There's lots of misunderstanding about the difference between shame and guilt when we're talking about sexuality. To me guilt is a good thing; it's a good emotion. Guilt doesn't feel good, but it's wonderful to feel because it reminds us that there is a remedy to get out of that guilty feeling. Because we agree that what we did was wrong, we repent and receive forgiveness; we confess and receive healing; we can make things right with another person; we can make things right with God. Then guilt has served the purpose, and it goes away.

God teaches us in His Word that guilt is for a purpose. It's for reminding us that we have violated His laws or our values—our laws. Guilt has a remedy. For example, King David says, "Restore to me again the joy of my salvation." After guilt has served its purpose, there has been a confession of sin and repentance, and then we're restored to feeling okay about ourselves.

On the other hand, shame never goes away because shame points at the person, and shame is about the person. Where guilt is about the behavior, shame would say, "I am a mistake." Where guilt would say, "I made a mistake," shame would say, "I'm a bad person for doing what I did." Where guilt would remind me that I need to take care of the problem, shame comes in the form of lies and accusations.

Shame continues to dig the hole deeper and deeper to make me feel like a bad person. Shame would suggest that people would not love me if they knew. Shame would suggest that I am going to be isolated, unloved, unvalued because of what I have done. Again, guilt would just convict me that what I'm doing is inconsistent with God's rules and my values. Guilt is a wonderful thing, if we understand it properly and pay attention to it as a potentially helpful emotion.[xii]

As I've said above, when we sin, the evil one and accuser attacks us with shame and accusations. Shame sounds like, "You are no good! You are a lousy Christian! I told you that you could not measure up!"

Mud Pies

Suppose you and a friend are at a large party with many guests. All of a sudden someone runs by and hits your friend in the face with a mud pie. After the initial shock, your friend panics and doesn't know what to do. So she slips behind the living room drapes to hide the mud on her face. You go to her and ask, "Why don't you go to the bathroom and wash it off?" She is terrified at the thought and says, "What if the host of the party sees me with this mud on my face? I can't risk it, I can't go and wash it off!"

What sense would that make to you? None! But that is how shame works. **We don't go and get cleaned up because we don't want to look dirty.** Never mind the fact the host of the party was there and saw the attack. You see God already knows that we screwed up. It comes as no surprise to Him; in fact He already forgave us for it. All we have to do is come to Him and admit it, and He will clean us up. Having a lot of shame about it is just a trick to get us not to clean up.

Shame is an attack on who we are, and it drives us away from God. Guilt (real guilt) drives us to God to get cleaned up. How do we fight accusations of shame? By renouncing the specific lies in Jesus' name... out loud. Repeat this out loud: *"I reject the lie that I do not measure up to being a good Christian, and I accept the truth that I don't need to measure up, that Jesus measures up for me and I am in Him."*

Important Stuff

"When we wallow in guilt, remorse, and shame over real or imagined sins of the past we are disdaining God's gift of grace.

"Preoccupation with self is always a major component of unhealthy guilt and recrimination. It stirs our emotions, churning in self-destructive ways, closes us in upon the mighty citadel of self, leads to depression and despair and preempts the presence of a compassionate God. The language of unhealthy guilt is harsh. It is demanding, abusing, criticizing,

We sometimes act like our failures can overcome the grace of God... Absolutely not true. In fact, it is the opposite! "But where sin is increased, grace increased all the more (Romans 5:20 NIV)."

rejecting, accusing, blaming, condemning, reproaching, and scolding. It is one of impatience and chastisement. Christians are shocked and horrified because they have failed. Unhealthy guilt becomes bigger than life. The image of the childhood story "Chicken Little" comes to mind. Guilt becomes the experience in which people feel the sky is falling.

Yes, we feel guilt over sins, but healthy guilt is one which acknowledges the wrong done and feels remorse, but is free to embrace the forgiveness that has been offered. Healthy guilt focuses on the realization that all has been forgiven, the wrong has been redeemed." [xiii] Brennan Manning

Whenever someone asks me, "What is the biggest life lesson you learned after going through LFL?" my mind always goes straight to how much my life has changed by understanding forgiveness more. It was very freeing for me to hear I am already forgiven, and I don't need to ask for forgiveness; rather, repentance is what I do because I am forgiven.

Like anyone, there have been people in my life who have hurt me, let me down or not met my needs. Sometimes the ways I was hurt seemed very small, but they built up inside me. I would convince myself the little ways I've been hurt didn't matter and didn't affect me.

After reading this chapter on forgiveness I did one of the Steps to Freedom. In this step, one thing I did was write down a list of people who I needed to forgive. At first it was hard to think of people who had hurt me because of the way I told myself that I'm strong and shouldn't be hurt by little things. Jesus asks us to forgive one another as we have been forgiven. Choosing not to forgive other people because I thought I was being strong comes out of a huge lie. I realized this lie when I started forgiving the people who came to my mind.

Jesus truly set me free when I chose to forgive, and He continues to free me more and more each day. There's such a huge difference in how I live my life now--I have a new perspective on things, and I've learned to love people more because of the forgiveness Jesus has given me.

Kristen

Lust: The Real Issue

Put to death, therefore, whatever belongs to your earthly nature: sexual immorality, impurity, lust, evil desires and greed, which is idolatry. (Colossians 3:5)

Concept

By this point in the book we should be learning that as we choose to step into the powerful freedom that Jesus offers us through His life, death and resurrection, we will no longer be slaves to our sinful nature. There are many different characteristics of our sinful nature, but due to the context of this book, we all know by now that we are focusing specifically on sexual sin. I want to break this all down and look at it in the light of some "hot topics" for us as Christian women. We all have our own specific "hot topics" when it comes to our sexuality, but the truth for all of us is that **LUST IS THE ISSUE!**

We can try throughout our lives to control our sexual desires physically in order to avoid sexual sin. We might have success much of the time, but it is important here to examine if our "success" was simply physical. For example, maybe your boundary to only go "so far" has held strong over and over again. Good for you! But let's look into your mind and spirit. Only you and God know if those are pure.

Our purity is so much deeper than our bodies! Maybe all the clothes stayed on, you didn't lie down, you only kissed for so long or you didn't kiss at all. Or maybe you struggle with the temptation to look at pornography, or you are controlled by your desire to masturbate. So you are able to resist and avoid whatever it is you struggle with—good for you! Those are big steps!

However, they are only a portion of the process involved in choosing not to be a slave to our sinful nature. In fact, maintaining physical boundaries alone can lead to bondage in other ways (pride, legalism, self-dependence, fear, isolation, etc.). Self-control and discipline are very important parts of our lives with God. In fact, self-control is one of the fruit of the Spirit (Galatians 5:23). So why do we struggle with it so much?

Could it be because we have "put the cart before the horse" (relying on our human self-control before we rely on God who empowers effective self-control)? With this in mind, picture it: God has created you to function as a vehicle of His glory. He has created you as a whole, functional being composed of your mind, body and spirit. You cannot be whole for Him as His temple (1 Corinthians 3:16) until every part of you (mind, body and spirit) has stepped into the freedom He offers you. Then, through the power of His Holy Spirit and with the authority He has given you, you fight with spiritual weapons and armor. He will fill you spiritually and, in turn, the power of temptation will be broken, and self-control will come much easier. Once again you will be walking in the victory that only comes through Christ Jesus—NOT THROUGH YOUR OWN POWER. (Read this again and discuss it with someone!)

Our spirit is at the very core of us. There are many experiences, thoughts, feelings and actions that make up the layers from our core all the way out to our outer layer (our body). As Christians, our desire is to be holy as He is holy (1 Peter 1:16) and to do what He calls us to do. However, there is this inner battle for our sexuality that we are often defeated by when it comes to our thought life and actions. So we think, "If I can just establish good enough boundaries and get the right people to ask the hard questions ("accountability" as we think of it), I will feel the infliction of shame when my answer isn't what it should be." Or we think, "If I just remain single and avoid the struggle altogether, I will be able to glorify God and will be a pure temple for His Holy Spirit—all because I have refined my self-control."

Like I said before, **self-control is essential.** However, when it's what we are ashamed of, fed up with and primarily focused on, we can assume we have been relying on ourselves in "our own strength" to resist the sinful nature. This cycle and way of life is defeating, hopeless and empty.

It is Christ who strengthens us (Philippians 4:13): **not just the thought of Christ, but the power spiritually that we have with Christ in us to fight and do battle against the devil's schemes to seek and destroy.** Our sexual boundaries will be solid and effective when they are birthed out of a free spirit and a pure mind. This does not mean we no longer have that sinful nature or that sexual sin is no longer a temptation. It simply means that we understand spiritually what has been offered to us (our identity), and we choose to step into that by taking our thoughts captive each time temptation comes our way. Then victory over darkness will be ours. Then self-control (what we wear, touch, look at, indulge in, talk about, walk like, buy, etc.) will come out of that victory naturally, because we truly desire it, and the strength will be ours as it's already been given to us.

Important Stuff

With all of this said, let's look at the title of this chapter: "LUST: THE REAL ISSUE." That is it! Period. What we do, what we wear, who we are with, etc., are all issues to be addressed if they are not edifying in some way, but they are likely just the symptoms of our sexual sin. At the very core of it all is the sin of lust, and for us as women that lust fuels so much of what we do. That is why we must target the lust and not the symptoms.

Try as we might to control, change and shame ourselves into purity, it does not work until we deal with the core spiritual issue—the sin of lust. Until we do that despair, hopelessness, shame and doubt will continue to nag at us, and we will still be in bondage.

Women, we have to learn to fight against our temptations spiritually first, remembering that the temptation is not the sin, it is what we do with that temptation that can become sin. We have the victory in Christ Jesus, so we have to fight like we do. We will find the things that once bound us no longer have power, and freedom will let us take a deep breath in victory. The next time temptation knocks on the door of our spirit, once again we must armor up and fight. **REMEMBER**: Lust is the issue! The rest of it is symptoms. Deal with the lust first, and the symptoms will fade. Why? Because they no longer have the power they once had.

Masturbation

Let's get specific about a symptom that is rarely talked about with women in a productive manner, and apply it to all that we have learned so far. This is a pretty sensitive subject that must be talked about among women as much as it is with men. Again, it is just one of the symptoms of lust that might be in your life, and it will look different than it does with men. The root of the habit reflects a stronghold. It is toxic, and we must talk about it boldly.

If you are a woman who has masturbated before or who struggles with it consistently, you are not alone. This is not talked about much among Christian women, which leaves us to feel very humiliated and abnormal. There is no need to feel either of those things, and there is no need to hide. God wants us to experience freedom from this and for us to bring it into the light of Christ that He might redeem us and make us new. The power we have in Christ Jesus can and will break this stronghold!

It is important you realize masturbating isn't the main problem. Of course, it probably isn't a healthy thing in your life, but it isn't the main problem. Once again, the sin is the lust. The key is figuring out what you are lusting for and where that comes from, then fighting against it spiritually first.

For most women, masturbation is different than it is for men. It is the same in that the goal is usually to achieve the sensation and "release" of an orgasm, but the reason for that desire in the first place is usually different. I have had many conversations with women about this, and we often discover that somewhere along the way they became aware of how their body works and that they can stimulate themselves. Of course, when that happens it easily takes on the form of a sin.

It isn't a sin because it feels good. As we now know, the way that God created our bodies to work is an amazing thing that we need to celebrate. It becomes a sin when it controls us, instead of us controlling it (Read 1 Corinthians 6:12). It becomes a sin when lust is involved. If we look hard enough, lust IS involved almost every time.

We can also make a good case against masturbation in that it can cause us to withhold sexually from our spouse. Even if you aren't married yet, this is something to consider because most people think the habit will go away once they are married. The problem is the root causes of masturbation go much deeper than just the physical process, and many women find that if they masturbated before being married, they still will after being married, because it continues to feed the stronghold that is still there.

For women, masturbation typically isn't fueled by visual images the same as it is for men. Sometimes this is the case, but it is more likely fueled by an emotional source. Fantasy is something that is often threaded throughout our lives as women. We fantasize and dream a lot, all in hopes of experiencing a feeling we're longing for, and physical stimulation naturally follows. The majority of the conversations I've had with women who struggle with masturbation reveal they do so because of habit. Often times there are no thoughts involved; it is just habit. But then other times it is rooted in fantasy. One way or another, women need to search to find the "root" that partners with the masturbation and deal with the root spiritually.

There are many reasons why a woman might lust and masturbate, but it is very important to separate the two. Talk openly with other women you trust about the source of the lust and to fight against it spiritually. As you fight spiritually against lust, the result will often be that masturbation does not happen as much, if at all anymore, because the power behind it has been taken away.

Fight Spiritually First

When we fight spiritually first, we receive sexual healing. God cleans up all the old sexual sin and closes the gates in our protective spiritual fence. Satan then does not have any legal rights or open gates to easily get at us. The next sexual temptation that comes at us will not have the power it once had because all the past sexual sins are gone—the strongholds have been broken. (You will be using *The Steps to Freedom in Christ* as a tool to break these strongholds after going through LFL.) The difference is amazing! Simply stated, use what you have learned so far about fighting the spiritual battle in our minds. Review the lessons if necessary. Reject the lies and thoughts verbally, and take the thoughts captive before Jesus.

Fight Emotionally Second

Many times our lust is not triggered by sexual thoughts or horniness; it is triggered by our emotions. We get into bad habits, like when we feel sad, insecure, bored, stressed or lonely, and we use lust and masturbation to feel better. Sometimes we use lust and masturbation like a drug, as a mood altering experience. One of the sad things about using this to help us through tough emotional times is that these are exactly the spots in life that Jesus wants to enter into with us. He wants us to depend on and look to Him when we're sad, lonely, frustrated, etc. If we learn to look to Jesus for our fulfillment during these emotional times, we can experience real satisfaction and growth.

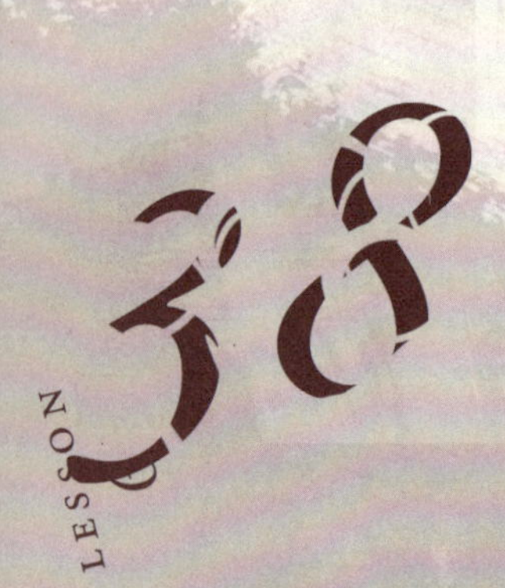

We must become aware of our emotions; ask the Holy Spirit to help you identify them. (I will use an example of feeling lonely, but you can substitute any other emotion in its place.) When we are lonely, and we use lust and masturbation to deal with that feeling, it is like using a drug. The mood alteration we achieve through lust and masturbation is short lived, and when we are done it hasn't helped with the loneliness. In fact, we usually feel worse because now we have to deal with our sinful lust on top of feeling lonely. It becomes a cycle of feeling lonely, lusting and masturbating, and feeling worthless and lonely again so we use lusting and masturbating again and so on.

To break this cycle, we need to learn how to deal with our emotions in a healthy way. One good way is to journal about them. Write down the feelings you experience before, during and after masturbating. If you are having trouble identifying what you are feeling, look at the Feelings Chart on page 96, and see which ones fit how you feel inside. Then bring your list to God in prayer, and ask Him to reveal to you anything He wants you to know. Don't forget to pause at this point—try to quiet your mind, and be still before the Lord so He can reveal things to you.

When we have actually dealt with our emotions, which were the real issue in the first place, the desire to masturbate almost always goes away, and we feel better. It is important to note, however, that almost all of our emotions come because of a thought we have. We think something and, in response, we feel something. Because this is the case, it becomes extremely important to identify what the initial thought was before the emotions come, so we can discern if the thought is based in God's truth—the truth of who we are in Christ. As we begin to respond faster to emotions in this way, we as women will spare ourselves a lot of emotional pain. This is a beautiful example of taking our thoughts captive to make them obedient to Christ (2 Corinthians 10:3–5).

Brainstorm with your fighting (accountability) partner or group about how they deal with emotions and what some things are you can do in the future. Remember that this takes work. It is hard to change old patterns, but God will teach you. It is worth the time and effort!

Fight Physically Third

Fighting physically third means the physical discipline of simply stopping yourself is your last responsibility. Our problem is we try this first, and failure happens over and over. Failure produces frustration, shame and defeat, and you remain stuck again and again. After you have taken care of the lust (the power behind the masturbation), and have dealt with your emotions in a healthy way (identifying the lies and replacing them with truth), it becomes much easier to stop masturbating. You must understand what needs to be stopped cold turkey is the lust. You must fight against that immediately and give no rights to Satan to bug you. Remember, lust is the issue!

I once had a conversation with a young woman who told me she was very frustrated with the role masturbation had played in her life. She shared that she had been doing it habitually for several years. After a long conversation about it, she was more frustrated. She said to me, "I honestly do not lust when I masturbate. If anything I am celebrating how cool it is and how creative God is while I am doing it." She admitted there are times when there is lustful "stuff" going on, but for the most part, her habit is strictly physical. She felt hopeless because she wanted to fight spiritually as the thoughts came and take care of the emotions that were fueling it. The problem was she couldn't see the lust and emotions clearly and was convinced they weren't even there.

We finally got to the bottom of it. She had been introduced to physical stimulus at a very young age by a family member. It was a very brief encounter, but it was the first time she was made aware of this part of her body. Naturally, as a child, she became very curious and began to innocently explore. It wasn't long after that she had childlike questions that went unanswered or silenced because they were "dirty." The emotions she had following that were humiliation, fear, confusion, loneliness, and the list went on. As she and I continued to talk, we both quickly realized that the reason she masturbated up to that day was because Satan had gotten a foothold into her life and spoken lies to her that said this part of her was dirty, out of control and something to hide. Once we saw that, we had a lot of fun replacing those lies with God's truth and celebrating how she was created. The power behind the years of habit was gone.

What she was convinced was just a physical habit that she felt hopeless about ended up being much deeper. Through much prayer, confession and worshiping of God's truth, masturbation began to take on a whole different role in her life. In times when she would normally be tempted to masturbate, she was able to journal out praises for how God created her and choose to believe the truth about who she is in Him. Now the physical desire quickly dwindles each time she does this, and it no longer controls her. This is just one story, but I hope it helps those of you who might have some of the same thoughts or feelings.

The truth is that for us as women, almost everything that goes on with us physically can be tied back to a thought that triggered an emotion. Because we have so many different emotions stemming from our thoughts, we can be sure that many of those thoughts are not based on God's truth about us. So as we come full circle, we find ourselves once again confronting our thoughts. It's time to stop giving in and "feeling" everything so much. We need to start praying, fighting and allowing our mind and emotions to be refined and used by God. We as women are so complex, intricate, beautiful and COOL! We don't have to live bound to our emotions. We can take our thoughts captive and live free in the truth.

Important Stuff

Always stay accountable; bring all thoughts and actions out into the light by talking and praying about them with each other. Talk about all your sexual thoughts, feelings and actions—positively celebrating the good ones and dealing with the negative ones. Also remember to take all thoughts to Jesus, good and bad.

THERE IS NO FEAR OR SHAME IN CHRIST JESUS OUR LORD AND SAVIOR!!

When I first sat down to write this, I realized that I had been editing things out in my mind to make it seem as though I have it together... like I followed a formula and now I don't struggle with lust anymore! That's not true--what is true is I am not in bondage to lust, because Jesus is more powerful than lust (sin), and I belong to him. It is also true that when I do mess up, I do not have to earn my way back to being in relationship with Him.

Lust has a number of symptoms in my life--being intrigued by sex scenes in movies (emotional and physical desire), pornography, messing around with my boyfriend, masturbation. The list could go on, but the symptoms aren't really even the problem here. The problem is what makes me want to do those things. What it comes down to is I bite into the lie, "Jesus is not enough." He won't provide an exciting romantic relationship for me so I have to go watch it instead. God doesn't love me enough to give me the pleasure and intimacy with a man I deserve, so if He won't give it to me, I'll just go take it from my boyfriend. Jesus is not enough of a comfort for me, so I'll choose to masturbate instead of going to Him. ALL LIES!

At a point of frustration in our relationship, my boyfriend and I sat down at a coffee shop and came up with a list of "No Trespassing Zones." We typed them up, put them where we'd remember to look at them, and subsequently broke nearly every item on the list by the end of the semester. The problem was because of our consistent decisions to choose our own way instead of God's, we were stuck in bondage to our sexual sin. Making a list of "no-nos" could not get us out of that hole. I couldn't begin to heal sexually because I was still under the influence of my past sexual sin. Satan had a bunch of open doors through which he could get to me.

At a Bible study, I learned about the way my thoughts and actions work together. First I think something, then I feel it and then I act on that feeling. It usually goes pretty quickly which is why I often miss the process and go straight to an action. It looks like this sometimes: Life is stressful so I have the thought that God is not enough to comfort me, so I feel anxious/stressed/defiant, and then I choose to

masturbate. When I slow that down and catch it in my mind, I can stop the whole thing at the thought that "God is not enough," because He has said that I am to find my rest in Him alone.

The physical control drop into place only after I have claimed my place as belonging to Jesus, have started fighting against the lies, and have acknowledged my thoughts and emotions. I use the term 'drops into place' because it is submissive and relaxed--not forced. My freedom, which comes from Christ alone, leads me to natural boundaries that are effective. It doesn't work the other way around. Creating boundaries and trying my hardest to stick to them will never lead me closer to freedom in Christ.

I still struggle; this isn't a one-time fix-it formula. But what is refreshing, relaxing and freeing is that I know God has provided a way out. I don't often get that yucky helpless and frustrated feeling anymore. I choose to believe the truth that I belong to Jesus who has power over sin and the evil ones. I believe that He is enough for me in all capacities, and because of that I can continue to grow in freedom sexually and in relationship with Him.

Katie

LESSON
7

He who conceals his sins does not prosper, but whoever confesses and renounces them finds mercy. (Proverbs 28:13)

Confess your sins to each other and pray for each other so that you may be healed. The earnest prayer of a righteous person has great power and produces wonderful results. (James 5:16 NLT)

Two people are better off than one, for they can help each other succeed. If one person falls, the other can reach out and help. But someone who falls alone is in real trouble. (Ecclesiastes 4:9–10 NLT)

Concept

Interdependence, not independence! We talk about accountability, but most of us don't know what it looks like. It's not just confession of all our yuck, yuck, yuck... it is not asking someone to be a cop to us. Accountability should never be a weight on our shoulders, holding us down or being a burden to bear.

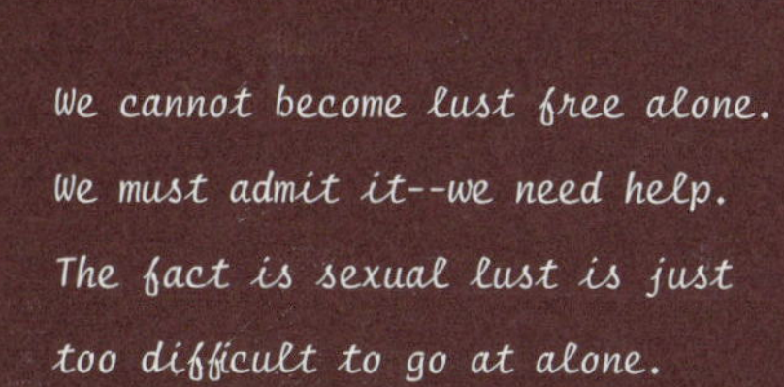

Accountability is a privilege; it's a protection from the enemy; it's for us to fight along side of others, warrior to warrior, watching each other's backs, encouraging and building each other up; picking each other up when we stumble and fall, side by side in the battle against our enemy.

Accountability means fostering vulnerable relationships that go deep into who we are as women and followers of Christ. This is absolutely necessary for maintaining our freedom in Christ and learning to live lust free. *"We absolutely need God and desperately need each other."* [xiv] **This is why we have the body of Christ (the Church, the body of believers). Read 1 Corinthians 12:14–27 and Romans 12:4–6 for more understanding.**

Fighting

We must choose to be accountable for all sexual issues (and all other issues in our lives). This is a critical part of the battle. Honesty in such a shameful area is tough, but staying in bondage to our sexual strongholds is much worse. We know how it feels to be caught in a sexual web of sin that tears us down and holds us there. Accountability is one step in the process of getting out of sexual bondage. This requires a lot of humility to be added to our relationships with one another, but the benefits are just too good to pass up!

Choose the people you are accountable with very carefully. Are they going to fight next to you? Do they understand the grace of God? Do they admit their failures? Have they experienced the relentless love of God firsthand? Have they encouraged you and built you up before? Are they trustworthy?

The apostles Paul and James and the book of Hebrews have some interesting things to say about this subject. Here are some quotes:

Dear brothers and sisters, if another believer is overcome by some sin, you who are godly should gently and humbly help that person back onto the right path. And be careful not to fall into the same temptation yourself. Share each other's burdens, and in this way obey the law of Christ (Galatians 6:1–2 NLT).

My dear brothers and sisters, if someone among you wanders away from the truth and is brought back, you can be sure that whoever brings the sinner back will save that person from death and bring about the forgiveness of many sins (James 5:19–20 NLT).

And let us consider how we may spur one another on toward love and good deeds. Let us not give up meeting together, as some are in the habit of doing, but let us encourage one another—and all the more as you see the Day approaching (Hebrews 10:24–25).

Putting Our Thoughts on the Table, Under the Light

There is a movie called *What Women Want.* It is about a man who could hear women's thoughts. They would think them, and he could hear them. He knew what they were thinking before they would say or do anything. Now that is an interesting gift! What would you do if someone you knew could hear everything you thought? It sure would make you vulnerable. All your thoughts, your secret thoughts and your secret sins would be out on the table with nothing hidden.

That's what it's like with Jesus and us. He hears our thoughts, good and bad. He knows what goes on in our heads. He already knows our secret thoughts and our lustful sins. He has already forgiven them! As Christians, Jesus calls us to a higher standard of living. He also wants our thoughts to sit out on the table in front of our sisters. He calls us to live in the light, and He wants our thoughts to live in the light. He calls us to share all our secret sins and pray with each other. He promises us that if we do, we will be healed.

When we choose to obey and share our sins, we become vulnerable to each other. When our thoughts are on the table in front of others and ourselves, something else significant happens. We gain the capacity to let go of them. We can then choose to shove them away from us and release them. We don't have to keep them hidden any longer—we can be free!

I know this is a difficult thing to do. However, I also know that it is much more difficult to live with the secret sexual sins and never deal with the strongholds they create.

I can't say this strongly enough: get and stay accountable to a gracious and loving person (or group), bringing everything you do into the light with them. Pray with them, and meet with them weekly if possible. Don't keep silent about your sins and failures—no matter what happens. Practicing active accountability will help you live in the light every day with Jesus and with your sisters in Christ! The healing will begin.

Ongoing Accountability

We now know to confess, renounce and accept our forgiveness from Jesus as soon as possible after the sin. This gives the enemy little chance to get at us through an open gate. We close it right away. We also have learned to confess and pray with our fighting partner as soon as possible, which brings spiritual and emotional healing. When we confess, we must do it honestly and in detail. Then before we pray use the following helps below:

First, ask Jesus to be with you and reveal to you and your fighting partner what issues you need to take care of. Then ask these questions of each other if you have sinned:

1. **What happened and where were you?** (Give all the necessary details, don't leave things out.)

2. **What were you thinking right before you did it?** (Confess anything and pray about these things if you need to.)

3. **Was there anything going through your mind earlier in the day that might have helped bring this on?** (If there is any thought that you should have taken captive earlier, confess that and deal with it now.)

4. **What were you feeling before you did it?** (Talk about healthy ways to deal with this emotion, and confess and renounce it if you used this sin to meet an emotional or other need.)

5. **Did any events happen to you today that led up to the sin?** (Deal with these events in the proper way now, and confess anything you need to in this area.)

6. **What lies do you think you were believing?** (If you were believing any lies before or after the sin, confess and renounce them using a Truth and Lie Statement: "In the wonderful name of Jesus, my Lord and Savior, I reject the lie that ________ and I accept the truth that ________.")

7. **Do you think you were deceived anytime during this process?** (If you see that you were, confess and renounce and accept your forgiveness.)

Renouncing, confessing, accepting forgiveness, and going against lies and deceit with truth and lie statements are the basics of choosing to be accountable and fighting with and for each other.

Repeat This Out Loud

"I, (insert your name), because I am a child of God and in the name of Jesus my Lord, choose now to live an accountable lifestyle. It is not forced on me; it is not asking someone to be a cop for me. I choose to fight with these women. I choose to deal honestly with my sins. I choose to stake myself next to them. I choose to pick them up when they fall and allow them to pick me up when I fall. I choose to live in the light. I choose to live in obedience to my Lord Jesus Christ, and I choose to allow His strength to flow through me to make this all possible."

We cannot win this battle alone; we must choose to use the Body of Christ in order to win this war. We must use our fighting partners.

This whole process is what I call the "Anti-Lust Updates." As we grow we will need to use our time together not just for sexual sins but also to be accountable for all issues that Jesus will bring to our minds. We begin to deal with much more than just the sexual stuff. We choose to live an accountable lifestyle. We choose to fight with and for each other. We choose to live in the light. No secret sins!

Unveil: True Stories

For a long time I struggled in silence with the sin of lust, with the main symptom for me being masturbation. I finished high school and went to college hoping things there would be different, hoping my sin wouldn't catch up to me. But I soon found the lust I had struggled with before was just as real and tempting as it had always been. I wanted to reach out, to tell someone how dead I felt inside. But fear and pride stopped me.

I remember back to the few times I had been brave in the past and shared my struggle. The reactions weren't ideal, and it still stung to remember their assumptions. "Girls don't struggle with that, what's wrong with you?" "Are you trying to say you're a lesbian?" "Why are you telling me this? It's weird." So I hid, isolating myself. I feared others would reject me if they knew the truth. My identity was wrapped in shame, because I thought lust defined me.

But after a while things got out of hand. I got depressed and couldn't keep up the facade. I hit my breaking point. I tried to think my way out of my problem. I researched and studied looking for a cure. But this only reinforced the lie that I was messed up, because a majority of the books I found on the subject were meant for men. I wondered if I was the only one. So I tried every other avenue I could think of, and eventually I was right back where I started--needing to talk.

That night I nervously told my roommate about my struggle. Once I started talking the words flooded out of me like someone had busted open a dam. It felt so good to be honest I forgot about her reaction. I closed my eyes and just enjoyed the freedom of the moment. When I finally opened my eyes I found the reaction was far from what I had imagined. My roommate had tears gushing down her face. And for the next several hours we talked. I came to find out I was not alone, and my struggle did not need to be a silent one.

The more I shared my story with other women, the more I saw walls crumble. Over and over I heard, "I thought I was the only one." Eventually, I met regularly with a group of LFL girls. And together we shared, cried, prayed and fought against the lies that fueled the sin, side by side. We became women warriors seeking the freedom only the truth can bring.

Libbie

Accountability changed my life. Not "accountability" as I had always known it--where people basically made me tell them my secrets, but accountability that gave me unconditional love, support and truth. As I began to walk this road of learning how to live lust free (as you are now), there were countless times I told myself I could open up to the people around me without telling them everything. I could let them get the general idea. Letting them into the deepest parts, the parts that have stuck with me for so long, wasn't necessary--not for me.

Thankfully God spoke to me through His Word and the girls in my LFL group. I had to admit I truly couldn't do it alone. I had been given sisters, fellow warriors. And so, almost paralyzed with fear and shame, I looked at the women in my group and told them the parts of my life Satan had control of. I told them the lies I believed for so long. I told them the areas I was broken in. Some things I had pushed so deep that I was shocked at even my own secrets.

As we went through LFL in the following weeks, I experienced healing and growth like I never imagined. My group reminded me I'm not what I have done; I am who God says I am--His child; I am in Christ and am worth the price of His life. Not only did they tell me that, they treated me like they actually believed it. I didn't get treated like a mistake, a basket case, a lost cause. I was treated as if I was of infinite worth and had the power of Christ in me.

I also found when I was completely vulnerable with the women in my group, they were completely vulnerable with me. I came alongside the very people supporting me and met them with grace and truth for their lives. Together we all realized we were no longer alone, ever.

To this day the women from my LFL group are so often God's voice of wisdom, love, truth and grace for me. They are strong for me when I feel weak. They allow me to say hard things to them. Together we discovered that complete vulnerability with fellow Christ-followers breaks Satan's power to isolate us in shame and strongholds, making us feel alone and weak. I am part of a family that together walked the road from brokenness, lies and shame to healing. Satan has no power over God's people when we are willing to truly fight spiritually and claim what is ours in Christ... forgiveness, new starts, truth, love, and ultimately freedom. Freedom!

For me the first step in the process was silencing Satan's voice that said I better not tell. Because I did open up I found warriors whose care for the state of my heart, mind and body were a tangible Jesus for me. Together we pushed each other toward healing and freedom. I've been healed in the deepest part of me, and I have lived the reality of Christ setting me free. Free from secrets, shame and Satan, and free to live as someone whose very identity is in belonging to Jesus Christ.

Erin

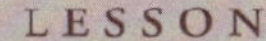

LESSON
8

Sexual Healing: Closing the Gates!

Confess your sins to each other and pray for each other so that you may be healed. The earnest prayer of a righteous person has great power and produces wonderful results. (James 5:16 NLT)

Concept

The Bible says that if we **do** confess to each other and pray for each other, **we will be healed**. A sure thing!

Don't confuse healing with forgiveness. Forgiveness is something that Jesus has already paid the price for and offers to us as a free gift. Forgiveness comes only through Jesus Christ and what he has done for us. We are talking about healing in this lesson.

Fighting

Picture a large fence that God creates around us when we accept Jesus as our Lord and Savior. A spiritual fence is erected to keep us safe from the enemy. As we live our lives from that point on, we sometimes sin. That sin opens a **gate** in our protective spiritual fence. Satan can use this open gate as a **legal right** to get at us, to accuse and bother us.

In the area of sexual lust, most of us have committed a lot of sins. Therefore we have opened many gates in our protective spiritual fence. The enemy uses these open gates to bind us (get us to believe lies) and establish spiritual strongholds in our lives. This lesson will help us close the gates so that healing can take place. In the name of our Savior, Jesus Christ, we will break the spiritual strongholds and receive healing.

Closing the Gates

The best tool I know of to help close the gates is *The Steps to Freedom in Christ,* by Neil T. Anderson. It helps us take a spiritual and moral inventory of our lives. We will concentrate on the sexual areas, but *The Steps to Freedom in Christ* can help us identify and destroy any spiritual strongholds.

Confessing our sins to each other can be tough. It takes guts and blatant honesty, but the process produces great freedom. (Hey, I bet that's why they call them *The Steps to Freedom in Christ*!) Also, working with others makes it easier for us to fight spiritually. We use *The Steps to Freedom in Christ* to guide us through the process of allowing Jesus to demolish our spiritual strongholds and close all the gates or legal rights Satan has access to in our lives.

Preparing to Do *The Steps to Freedom in Christ*

In my experience, doing *The Steps to Freedom in Christ* may take six to eight hours or more. I say this so you'll make sure to plan enough uninterrupted time. You might want to break it into several days. You will need to do it with your fighting (accountability) partner or group.

Sexual Junk: Don't deal with the sexual junk until you get to the second part of the sixth step. When you get to it, don't play games—be specific about the sins in your past. Make a list first, allowing God to bring up every sexual sin, so you can confess each one specifically. Break the sinful bond with each sin. After you've completed this process, you will be free from all the garbage and bondage connected with it. You will have closed the gates in your fence of spiritual protection. Shred your list... enjoy it and thank God for your freedom.

This is what I've seen over and over again: Those who have been specific to pray through each sin brought to their minds have broken the sinful bonds. They find tremendous freedom. If they ignored a sin that came to their mind during the confession time, it was easily used to tempt them again.

That's why we need to be specific and confess each image, experience, participation, practice, person, and habit. Confess <u>every sexual use</u> of our body we can remember so each sinful bond connected to lustful images, thoughts or actions can be broken and brought to Christ. Then we'll experience great freedom from the power of lust connected to those emotions, people and images. Truly closing the gates leads to great freedom!

After *The Steps to Freedom in Christ*, any lustful thoughts that come will be fresh ones, without the power of the old, habitual ones. In other words, lustful thoughts we replayed in our minds are gone. It's much easier to take new thoughts captive to Christ because they lack the old bondages. The legal rights Satan had are gone (the gates are closed). He'll still try to tempt you with those thoughts, but they won't have the same power as before. **This is what makes lust free living possible!**

Pray-ers: Both you and your accountability partner (or group) should ask at least three to five people to pray for you at the time you are going through *The Steps to Freedom in Christ.* Ask them to pray during the **specific time** you planned if possible. Pick people who you are sure will actually pray... people who are concerned about you and who love you.

When these things are in place you are ready to start *The Steps to Freedom in Christ.*

Sexual healing? Is there such a thing? I tried for many years to control my lustful thoughts and urges by myself and failed miserably, so I didn't think there was such a thing as "sexual healing." I failed because I didn't know how to fight spiritually with Jesus at my side. I didn't know I could. I went through life seeing myself as damaged and unworthy because of my sins. So, what would I do to try and feel better? Sin some more! Satan really kicked my butt for a very long time.

In my 42 years, I tried many self-help books, individual counseling, couple counseling, church and Bible studies. Nothing got through to me like the Lust Free Living study. It truly is a unique experience, and I feel like I finally "got it"! Going through the Steps to Freedom afterward was the KEY combination to finally confront, face and heal from all the sin and pain. I remembered things I had buried deep down from childhood. Having someone I trusted to go through the process of healing with me was so important. Everything suddenly became very real once confessed aloud.

I have learned everything I do is somehow spiritual and the only way to keep fighting against the efforts of the enemy is to live in the truth and the light rather than hide in darkness, as that is what feeds the enemy's power to affect me, and keeps him coming back for more. We need to know we are good enough just the way we are in Christ Jesus and fight!

Jas

Review Before Doing The Steps to Freedom in Christ

- Know and believe your real identity in Christ.
- Celebrate and enjoy how God has created us as women, including how we are sexually.
- Fight in the spiritual realm first. The other areas will be easier to deal with.
- Take lustful thoughts captive as soon as they come at you.
- We are a forgiven people; accept it and move toward Jesus—don't allow Satan to trick you into feeling that you cannot be forgiven. "A Saint is not someone who is good, but one who experiences the goodness of God." Thomas Merton
- Treat lust as the sin—deal with the physical and emotional areas progressively, step-by-step.
- Be accountable to someone who can love you in spite of your failures, just like Jesus does.
- Always close the gates in your fence of spiritual protection as soon as possible—use *The Steps to Freedom in Christ* and review it often.

Jesus looked at them intently and said, "Humanly speaking, it is impossible. But with God everything is possible" (Matthew 19:26 NLT).

We CAN live lust free lives!

If you've completed this program and have found it beneficial, e-mail Seashore@LFLgroup.org or Jamie@LFLgroup.org and tell us how things have changed in your life before and after you went through the program. Feel free to ask questions if you need extra help. We would really appreciate the encouragement of hearing your story.

Preparing for The Steps to Freedom in Christ

Focus on the right things.

Christianity is not a philosophy, a system of thought or way of living by not doing the wrong things. Christianity is a relationship with God the Father, Jesus His son and the Holy Spirit living in us. Our encounter with God is what makes these truths workable. It is our relationship with Him that gives us the authority to live lives that are not only lust free but free from all strongholds. Following the principles in this book is worthless unless we have an encounter with the living God. Seek Him and you will find Him—that is His promise, keep seeking. We must not get hung up on "doing" these principles. We must get hung up on submitting and knowing God through Jesus the Anointed One. Keep our eyes, minds and ears on Jesus and these truths will come alive in your heart. LFL is worthless without Jesus and our relationship with Him.

It's a process, a start down the road, not a cure.

The process is just getting started when your LFL group completes the workbooks. Although the fighting will never end, you will get better at it if you don't give up. Continue to allow Jesus to renew your mind with the Holy Spirit's power in you. Don't give up ever, Jesus will walk you into freedom; it's a promise.

Make sure you finish *The Steps to Freedom in Christ.*

This is a critical issue. You must finish *The Steps to Freedom in Christ*, and it is always most effective to do it with someone else, hopefully your fighting partner. This is the best way to close all the past open gates and begin to get rid of all the strongholds in your life.

Use this tool over and over again as you continue to fight spiritually.

The Steps to Freedom in Christ is a great tool for you to use as God directs you. Neil T. Anderson says it is like peeling an onion; it comes off in layers as God moves in our lives. I personally have gone through *The Steps to Freedom in Christ* hundreds of times with other people, and the Holy Spirit prompted me to deal with things in my life even up to the 32nd time.

You will sin lustfully again even after the LFL process has begun.

You know the honeymoon is over when you find yourself returning to old behaviors after being pure for a while. Don't be surprised when the same old feelings, shame and lies come at you like before. The battle intensifies here; the enemy will try his best to keep you in shame. "See, it did not work for you! It does not work at all! You are still a screw up and always will be! You aren't good enough to call yourself a Christian!" Again, lies, lies and more lies from the father of lies and his cohorts. Absolutely don't fall for this—start choosing to live an accountable lifestyle. Go to your fighting partner(s) immediately and confess, pray and repent. Don't fall for this one, and if you have, take care of it now with a truth-and-lie statement.

Don't allow any sin to go unconfessed—close the gates immediately.

Being just plain lazy gets some of us in trouble later on. We get sloppy and don't deal with sin immediately. We sometimes get lazy when we should remain vigilant about taking thoughts captive. If this is happening to you, talk to your fighting partner about it, and remember you are in a war zone. Ed Welch said it this way, "The only possible attitude toward out-of-control desire is a declaration of all-out war… There is something about war that sharpens the senses… You hear a twig snap or the rustling of leaves, and you are in attack mode. Someone coughs and you are ready to pull the trigger. Even after days of little or no sleep, war keeps us vigilant."[XV]

Confess and renounce your sins specifically.

Failure to do this will make accountability empty and not real. Don't allow fear and shame to stop you from putting everything on the table with your fighting partner.

Don't have a good fighting partner?

Remember we really need to choose our fighting partner carefully. Choose someone who is willing to be honest with you, someone who has a high degree of integrity. I suggest you go through LFL with your friends so you can pick your fighting partner from among your friends. If this did not happen, take your friends through LFL and help them deal with their sexual sin also. It usually works best if your fighting partner is in close proximity geographically so you can get together often, but this is not necessary.

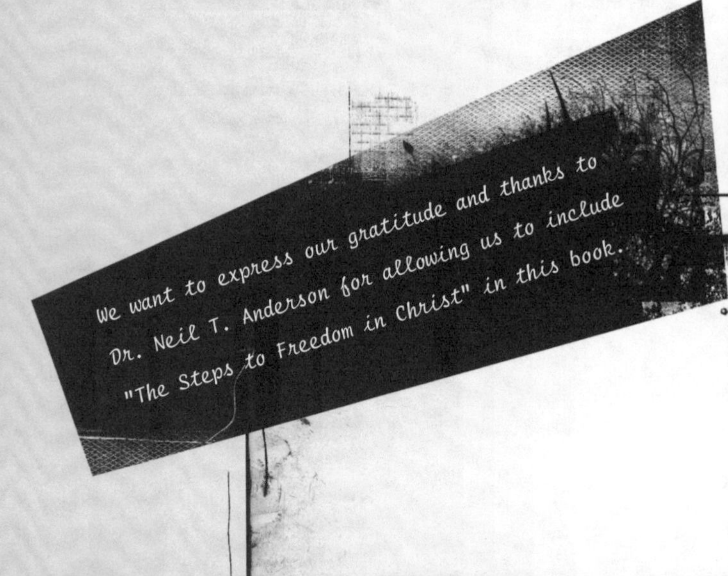

The Steps to Freedom in Christ

by Dr. Neil T. Anderson

The Whole Gospel

God created Adam and Eve to be spiritually alive, which means that their souls were in union with God. Living in a dependent relationship with their Heavenly Father, they were to exercise dominion over the earth. Acting independently of God, they chose to disobey Him and their choice to sin separated them from God. Consequently, all their descendents are born physically alive, but spiritually dead, i.e. separated from God. Since we have all sinned and fallen short of the glory of God (Romans 3:23), we remain separated from Him and cannot fulfill the original purpose for our creation, which is to glorify God and enjoy His presence forever. Satan became the rebel holder of authority, and the god of this world. Jesus referred to him as the ruler of this world, and the Apostle John wrote that the whole world lies in the power of the evil one (1 John 5:19).

Jesus came to undo the works of Satan (1 John 3:8), and take upon Himself the sins of the world. By dying for our sins, Jesus removed the enmity that existed between God and those He created in His image. The resurrection of Christ brought new life to those who put their trust in Him. Every born-again believer's soul is again in union with God and that is most often communicated in the New Testament as being "in Christ," or "in Him." The Apostle Paul explained that anyone who is *in Christ* is a new creation (2 Corinthians 5:17). The Apostle John wrote, *But as many as received Him, to them He gave the right to become children of God, to those who believe in His name* (John 1:12), and he also wrote, *See how great a love the Father has bestowed on us, that we would be called children of God; and such we are* (1 John 3:1).

No amount of effort on your part can save you, and neither can any religious activity no matter how well intentioned. We are saved by faith and by faith alone. All that remains for us to do is put our trust in the finished work of Christ. *For by grace you have been saved through faith; and that not of yourself, it is a gift of God; not as a result of works, so that no one may boast* (Ephesians 2:8–9). If you have never received Christ, you can do so right now. God knows the thoughts and intentions of your heart, so all you have to do is put your trust in God alone. You can express your decision in prayer as follows:

> *Dear heavenly Father, thank you for sending Jesus to die on the cross for my sins. I acknowledge that I have sinned and that I cannot save myself. I believe that Jesus came to give me life and by faith I now choose to receive You into my life as my Lord and Savior. May the power of your indwelling presence enable me to be the person You created me to be. I pray that You would grant me repentance leading to a knowledge of the truth so that I can experience my freedom in Christ and be transformed by the renewing of my mind. In Jesus' precious name I pray. Amen*

Assurance of Salvation

Paul wrote, "If you confess with your mouth Jesus as Lord, and believe in your heart that God raised Him from the dead, you will be saved" (Romans 10:9). Do you believe that God the Father raised Jesus from the dead? Did you invite Jesus to be your Lord and Savior? Then you are a child of God and nothing can separate you from the love of Christ (Romans 8:35). Your Heavenly Father has sent His Holy Spirit to live within you and bear witness with your spirit that you are a child of God (Romans 8:16). *You were sealed* ***in Him*** *with the Holy Spirit of promise* (Ephesians 1:13). The Holy Spirit will guide you into all truth (John 16:13).

Resolving Personal and Spiritual Conflicts

Since we are all born dead (spiritually) in our trespasses and sin (Ephesians 2:1), we had neither the presence of God in our lives nor the knowledge of His ways. Consequently, we all learned to live our lives independent of God. When we became new creations in Christ our minds were not instantly renewed. That is why Paul wrote, *Do not conform any longer to the pattern of this world, but be transformed by the renewing of your mind. Then you will be able to test and approve what God's will is—His good, pleasing, and perfect will* (Romans 12:2 NIV). That is why new Christians struggle with many of the same old thoughts and habits. Their minds have been previously programmed to live independently of God and that is the chief characteristic of our old nature or flesh. As new creations in Christ we have the mind of Christ and the Holy Spirit will lead us into all truth.

To experience our freedom in Christ and grow in the grace of God requires repentance, which literally means a change of mind. Repentance is not something we can do on our own, therefore we need to submit to God and resist the devil (James 4:7). The Steps to Freedom In Christ (Steps) are designed to help you do that. Submitting to God is the critical issue. He is the wonderful counselor and the One who grants repentance leading to a knowledge of the truth (2 Timothy 2:24–26). The Steps cover seven critical issues between ourselves and God. We will not experience our freedom in Christ if we seek false guidance, believe lies, fail to forgive others as we have been forgiven, live in rebellion, respond in pride, fail to acknowledge our sin, and continue in the sins of our ancestors. *He who conceals transgressions will not prosper, but he who confesses and forsakes [renounces] them will find compassion* (Proverbs 28:13). *Therefore, since we have this ministry, as we received mercy, we do not lose heart, but we renounced the things hidden because of shame, not walking in craftiness or adulterating the word of God, but by the manifestation of truth* (2 Corinthians 4:1–2).

Even though Satan is defeated, he still rules this world through a hierarchy of demons who tempt, accuse, and deceive those who fail to put on the armor of God, stand firm in their faith, and take every thought captive to the obedience of Christ. Our sanctuary is our identity and position in Christ and we have all the protection we need to live a victorious life, but if we fail to assume our responsibility and give ground to Satan, we will suffer the consequences of our sinful attitudes and actions. The good news is, we can repent and reclaim all that we have in Christ, and that is what the Steps will enable you to do.

Processing the Steps

Ideally, it would be best if you read *Victory Over the Darkness,* and *The Bondage Breaker* before you processed the Steps. Audio books and tapes are also available from Freedom In Christ Ministries. The best way to go through the Steps is to process them with a trained encourager. The book, *Discipleship Counseling,* explains the theology and process. You can also go through the Steps on your own. Every step is explained so you will have no trouble doing that. I suggest you find a quiet place where you can process the Steps out loud. If you experience some mental interference, just ignore it and continue on. Thoughts like, *This isn't going to work*, or *I don't believe this*, or blasphemous, condemning, and accusing thoughts have no power over you unless you believe them. It is just a thought and it doesn't make any difference if it originates from yourself, an external source, or from Satan and his demons. It will be resolved when you have fully repented. If you are working with a trained encourager, share any mental or physical opposition that you are experiencing. The mind is the control center, and you will not lose control in the counseling session if you don't lose control of your mind. The best way to do that, if you are being mentally harassed, is to just share it. Exposing the lies to the light breaks the power.

Remember, you are child of God and seated with Christ in the heavenlies. That means you have the authority and power to do His will. The Steps don't set you free. Jesus sets you free and you will progressively experience that freedom as you respond to Him in faith and repentance. Don't worry about any demonic interference; most do not experience any. It doesn't make any difference if Satan has a little role or a bigger role, the critical issue is your relationship with God and that is what you are resolving. This is a ministry of reconciliation. Once those issues are resolved, Satan has no right to remain. Successfully completing this repentance process is not an end, it is a beginning of growth. Unless these issues are resolved, however, the growth process will be stalled and your Christian life will be stagnant.

Preparation

Processing these Steps can play a major role in your continuing process of discipleship. The purpose is to get you firmly rooted in Christ. It doesn't take long to establish your identity and freedom in Christ, but there is no such thing as instant maturity. Renewing your mind and conforming to the image of God is a lifelong process. May the Lord grace you with His presence as you seek to do His will. Once you have experienced your freedom in Christ you can help others experience the joy of their salvation. Begin the Steps with the following prayer and declaration.

Prayer

Dear heavenly Father, You are present in this room and in my life. You alone are all-knowing, all-powerful and everywhere present and I worship You alone. I declare my dependency upon You, for apart from You I can do nothing. I choose to believe your Word, which teaches that all authority in heaven and earth belongs to the resurrected Christ, and being alive in Christ I have the authority to resist the devil as I submit to You. I ask that You fill me with Your Holy Spirit and guide me into all truth. I ask for your complete protection and guidance as I seek to know You and do your will. In the wonderful name of Jesus I pray. Amen.

Declaration

In the name and authority of the Lord Jesus Christ I command Satan and all evil spirits to release their hold on me in order that I can be free to know and choose to do the will of God. As a child of God who is seated with Christ in the heavenly places, I declare that every enemy of the Lord Jesus Christ in my presence be bound. Satan and all his demons cannot inflict any pain or in any way prevent God's will from being done in my life today, because I belong to the Lord Jesus Christ.

Review of Your Life

Before going through the "Steps to Freedom in Christ," review the following events of your life to discern specific areas that need to be addressed.

Family History

- ❑ Religious history of parents and grandparents
- ❑ Home life from childhood through high school
- ❑ History of physical or emotional illness in the family
- ❑ Adoption, foster care, guardians

Personal History

- ❑ Eating habits (bulimia, anorexia, compulsive eating)
- ❑ Addictions (smoking, drugs, alcohol)
- ❑ Prescription medications (what for?)
- ❑ Sleeping patterns, dreams and nightmares
- ❑ Rape or any other sexual, physical or emotional abuse
- ❑ Thought life (obsessive, blasphemous, condemning and distracting thoughts, poor concentration, fantasy, suicidal, fearful, jealous, confused, guilt and shame)
- ❑ Mental interference during church, prayer or Bible study
- ❑ Emotional life (anger, anxiety, depression, bitterness, and fear)
- ❑ Spiritual journey (salvation: when, how, and assurance)

Step One

COUNTERFEIT VS. REAL

The first step toward experiencing your freedom in Christ is to renounce (verbally reject) all involvement (past or present) with occult, cult or false religious teachings or practices. Participation in any group that denies that Jesus Christ is Lord and/or elevates any teaching or book to the level of (or above) the Bible must be renounced. In addition, groups that require dark, secret initiations, ceremonies, vows, pacts or covenants need to be renounced. God does not take lightly false guidance. '*As for the person who turns to mediums and to spiritists... I will also set My face against that person and will cut him off from among his people*' (Leviticus 20:6). Since you don't want the Lord to cut you off, ask Him to guide you as follows:

> *Dear heavenly Father, please bring to my mind anything and everything that I have done knowingly or unknowingly that involves occult, cult or false religious teachings or practices. I want to experience your freedom by renouncing any and all false guidance. In Jesus' name I pray. Amen.*

The Lord may bring things to your mind that you had forgotten, even things you participated in as a game or thought was a joke. You might even have been passively yet curiously watching others participate in counterfeit religious practices. The purpose is to renounce all counterfeit spiritual experiences and their beliefs.

To help bring these things to your mind, prayerfully consider the following *Non-Christian Spiritual Checklist.* Then pray the prayer following the checklist to renounce each activity or group the Lord brings to mind. He may reveal to you ones that are not on the list. Be especially aware of your need to renounce non-Christian folk religious practices if you have grown up in another culture. It is important that you prayerfully renounce them **out loud**.

Non-Christian Spiritual Checklist

(Check all those that you have participated in.)

- ❑ Out of body experience
- ❑ Ouija board
- ❑ Bloody Mary
- ❑ Occult games
- ❑ Magic Eight Ball
- ❑ Spells or curses
- ❑ Mental telepathy/control
- ❑ Automatic writing
- ❑ Trances
- ❑ Spirit guides
- ❑ Fortune telling/divination
- ❑ Tarot cards
- ❑ Levitation
- ❑ Witchcraft/wicca/sorcery
- ❑ Satanism
- ❑ Palm reading
- ❑ Astrology/horoscopes
- ❑ Hypnosis
- ❑ Astral projection
- ❑ Seances/mediums/channelers
- ❑ Black or white magic
- ❑ Blood pacts
- ❑ Fetishism/crystals/charms
- ❑ Sexual spirits
- ❑ Martial arts (mysticism)
- ❑ Superstitions
- ❑ Silva Mind Control
- ❑ Mormonism (Latter-Day Saints)
- ❑ Jehovah's Witness
- ❑ New Age (teachings, medicine)
- ❑ Masons
- ❑ Christian Science/Mind Science
- ❑ Unification Church (Moonies)
- ❑ The Forum (EST)
- ❑ Church of Scientology
- ❑ Unitarianism/Universalism
- ❑ Transcendental Meditation
- ❑ Yoga (religion, not exercise)
- ❑ Hare Krishna
- ❑ Bahaism
- ❑ Native American spirit worship
- ❑ Islam
- ❑ Hinduism
- ❑ Buddhism (including Zen)
- ❑ Black Muslim
- ❑ Rosicrucianism
- ❑ False gods (money, sex, power, pleasure, certain people)
- ❑ Other (non-Christian religions; cults; movies; music; books; video games; comics or fantasy games that glorify Satan, which precipitated nightmares or mental battles; and all other questionable experiences including spiritual visitations and nightmares)

Additional questions to help you become aware of counterfeit religious experiences

1. Do you now have, or have you ever had, an imaginary friend, spirit guide, or "angel" offering you guidance or companionship? (If it has a name, renounce it by name.)
2. Have you ever heard voices in your head or had repeating, nagging thoughts such as "I'm dumb," "I'm ugly," "Nobody loves me," "I can't do anything right"—as if there were a conversation going on inside your head?
3. Have you ever been hypnotized, attended a New Age seminar, or consulted a medium or spiritist?
4. Have you ever made a secret vow or pact (or inner vow, e.g., "I will never...")?
5. Have you ever been involved in a satanic ritual or attended a concert where Satan was the focus?

Once you have completed your checklist and the questions, confess and renounce every false religious practice, belief, ceremony, vow or pact that you were involved in by praying the following prayer aloud:

> *Lord Jesus, I confess that I have participated in* (specifically name every belief and involvement with all that you have checked above) *and I renounce them all as counterfeits. I pray that You will fill me with Your Holy Spirit that I may be guided by You. Thank You that in Christ I am forgiven. Amen.*

Satanic Worship

People who have been subjected to Satanic Ritual Abuse (SRA) need the help of someone who understands dissociative disorders and spiritual warfare. If you have been involved in any form of satanic worship say aloud the following "Special Renunciations." Read across the page, renouncing the first item in the column under "Kingdom of Darkness," and then announcing the truth in the column under "Kingdom of Light." Continue down the page in that manner. Notice that satanic worship is the antithesis of true worship.

Kingdom of Darkness	*Kingdom of Light*
I renounce ever signing my name over to Satan or having my name signed over to Satan.	I announce my name is now written in the Lamb's book of life.
I renounce any ceremony in which I have been wed to Satan.	I announce I am the bride of Christ.
I renounce any and all covenants I made with Satan.	I announce I'm under the new covenant with Christ.
I renounce all satanic assignments for my life, including duties, marriage, and children.	I announce and commit myself to know and obey only the will of God and accept only His guidance.
I renounce all spirit guides assigned to me.	I accept only the leading of the Holy Spirit.
I renounce ever giving my blood in the service of Satan.	I trust only the blood of the Lord Jesus Christ.
I renounce ever eating flesh or drinking blood for satanic worship.	By faith I symbolically eat only the flesh and drink only the blood of Jesus in Holy Communion.
I renounce any and all guardians and satanic parents who were assigned to me.	I announce God is my Father and the Holy Spirit is my guardian by whom I am sealed.
I renounce any baptism whereby I have been identified with Satan.	I announce I have been baptized into Christ Jesus.
I renounce any and all sacrifices that were made on my behalf by which Satan may claim ownership of me.	I announce only the sacrifice of Christ has any hold on me. I belong to Him. I have been purchased by the blood of the Lamb.

Step Two

DECEPTION VS. TRUTH

The Christian life is lived by faith according to what God says is true. Jesus is the truth, the Holy Spirit is the Spirit of truth, God's word is truth and we are to speak the truth in love (see John 14:6; 16:13; 17:17; Ephesians 4:15). The biblical response to truth is *faith* regardless of whether we *feel* it is true or not. In addition, Christians are to have no part in lying, deceiving, stretching the truth, or anything else associated with falsehood. Lies keep us in bondage, but it is the truth that sets us free (John 8:32). David wrote, *How blessed [happy] is the man... in whose spirit there is no deceit* (Psalm 32:2). Joy and freedom come from walking in the truth.

We find the strength to walk in the light of honesty and transparency before God and others (see 1 John 1:7) when we know that God loves and accepts us just as we are. We can face reality, acknowledge our sins and not try to hide. Begin this commitment to truth by praying the following prayer out loud. Don't let any opposing thoughts such as *This is a waste of time* or *I wish I could believe this, but I can't,* keep you from pressing forward. God will strengthen you as you rely on Him.

> *Dear heavenly Father, You are the truth and I desire to live by faith according to Your truth. The truth will set me free, but in many ways I have been deceived by the father of lies, the philosophies of this fallen world, and I have deceived myself. I choose to walk in the light, knowing that You love and accept me just as I am. As I consider areas of possible deception, I invite the Spirit of truth to guide me into all truth. Please protect me from all deception as You "search me, O God, and know my heart; try me and know my anxious thoughts; and see if there be any hurtful way in me, and lead me in the everlasting way" (Psalm 139:23–24). In the name of Jesus I pray. Amen.*

Prayerfully consider the lists in the three exercises below, using the prayers at the end of each exercise in order to confess any ways you have given in to deception or wrongly defended yourself. You cannot instantly renew your mind, but the process will never get started without acknowledging our mental strongholds or defense mechanisms, which are sometimes called flesh patterns.

Ways You Can Be Deceived by the World

- ❑ Believing that acquiring money and things will bring lasting happiness (Matthew 13:22; 1 Timothy 6:10)
- ❑ Believing that excessive food and alcohol can relieve my stress and make me happy (Proverbs 23:19–21)
- ❑ Believing that an attractive body and personality will get me what I need (Proverbs 31:10; 1 Peter 3:3–4)
- ❑ Believing that gratifying sexual lust will bring lasting satisfaction (Ephesians 4:22; 1 Peter 2:11)

- ❑ Believing that I can sin and get away without any negative consequences (Hebrews 3:12–13)
- ❑ Believing that I need more than what God has given me in Christ (2 Corinthians 11:2–4,13–15)
- ❑ Believing that I can do whatever I want and no one can touch me (Proverbs 16:18; Obadiah 3;1 Peter 5:5)
- ❑ Believing that unrighteous people who refuse to accept Christ go to heaven anyway (1 Corinthians 6:9–11)
- ❑ Believing that I can associate with bad company and not become corrupted (1 Corinthians 15:33–34)
- ❑ Believing that I can read, see, or listen to anything and not be corrupted (Proverbs 4:23–27; Matthew 5:28)
- ❑ Believing that there are no consequences on earth for my sin (Galatians 6:7–8)
- ❑ Believing that I must gain the approval of certain people in order to be happy (Galatians 1:10)
- ❑ Believing that I must measure up to certain standards in order to feel good about myself (Galatians 3:2–3; 5:1)

Lord Jesus, I confess that I have been deceived by (confess the items you checked above). *I thank You for Your forgiveness, and I commit myself to believe only Your truth. In Jesus' name I pray. Amen.*

Ways to Deceive Yourself

- ❑ Hearing God's Word but not doing what it says (James 1:22)
- ❑ Saying I have no sin (1 John 1:8)
- ❑ Thinking I am something I'm really not (Galatians 6:3)
- ❑ Thinking I am wise in this worldly age (1 Corinthians 3:18–19)
- ❑ Thinking I can be truly religious but not bridle my tongue (James 1:26)
- ❑ Thinking that God is the source of my problems (Lamentations 3)
- ❑ Thinking I can live my life without the help of anyone else (1 Corinthians 12:14–20)

Lord Jesus, I confess that I have deceived myself by (confess the items checked above). *Thank You for Your forgiveness. I commit myself to believe only Your truth. In Jesus' name I pray. Amen.*

Ways to Wrongly Defend Yourself

- ❑ Denial of reality (conscious or unconscious)
- ❑ Fantasy (escaping reality by daydreaming, TV, movies, music, computer or video games, drugs, alcohol)
- ❑ Emotional insulation (withdrawing from people or keeping people at a distance to avoid rejection)
- ❑ Regression (reverting back to less threatening times)
- ❑ Displaced anger (taking out frustrations on innocent people)

❑ Projection (attributing to another what you find unacceptable in yourself)
❑ Rationalization (making excuses for my own poor behavior)
❑ Lying (Protecting self through falsehoods)
❑ Blaming myself (when not responsible) and others
❑ Hypocrisy (presenting a false image)

> *Lord Jesus, I confess that I have wrongly defended myself by* (confess the items checked above). *Thank You for Your forgiveness. I trust You to defend and protect me. In Jesus' name I pray. Amen.*

The wrong ways we have employed to shield ourselves from pain and rejection are often deeply engrained in our lives. You may need additional discipling/counseling to learn how to allow Christ to be your rock, fortress, deliverer and refuge (see Psalm 18:1–2). The more you learn how loving, powerful, and protective God is, the more you'll be likely to trust Him. The more you realize His complete acceptance of you in Christ, the more you'll be released to be open, honest and (in a healthy way) vulnerable before God and others.

The New Age movement has twisted the concept of faith by teaching that we make something true by believing it. That is false. We cannot create reality with our minds; only God can do that. Our responsibility is to *face* reality and choose to believe what God says is true. True biblical faith, therefore, is choosing to believe and act upon what is true, because God has said it is true, and He is the Truth. Faith is something you decide to do, not something you feel like doing. Believing something doesn't make it true; *it's already true, therefore we choose to believe it!* Truth is not conditioned by whether we choose to believe it or not.

Everybody lives by faith. The only difference between Christian faith and non-Christian faith is the object of our faith. If the object of our faith is not trustworthy, then no amount of believing will change that. That's why our faith must be grounded on the solid rock of God's perfect, unchanging character and the truth of His word. For two thousand years Christians have known the importance of verbally and publicly declaring truth. Read aloud the following Statements of Truth, and carefully consider what you are professing. You may find it helpful to read it aloud daily for several weeks, which will help renew your mind to the truth.

Statements of Truth

1. *I recognize there is only one true and living God who exists as the Father, Son, and Holy Spirit. He is worthy of all honor, praise, and glory as the One who made all things and holds all things together.* (See Exodus 20:2–3; Colossians 1:16–17.)

2. *I recognize Jesus Christ is the Messiah, the Word who became flesh and dwelt among us. I believe He came to destroy the works of the devil, and that He disarmed the rulers and authorities and made a public display of them, having triumphed over them.* (See John 1:1,14; Colossians 2:15; 1 John 3:8.)

3. *I believe God demonstrated His own love for me in that while I was still a sinner, Christ died for me. I believe He has delivered me from the domain of darkness and transferred me to His kingdom, and in Him I have redemption, the forgiveness of sins.* (See Romans 5:8; Colossians 1:13–14.)

4. *I believe I am now a child of God, and I am seated with Christ in the heavenlies. I believe I was saved by the grace of God through faith, and it was a gift and not a result of any works on my part.* (See Ephesians 2:6,8–9; 1 John 3:1–3.)

5. *I choose to be strong in the Lord and in the strength of His might. I put no confidence in the flesh, for the weapons of warfare are not of the flesh but are divinely powerful for the destruction of strongholds. I put on the full armor of God. I resolve to stand firm in my faith and resist the evil one.* (See 2 Corinthians 10:4; Ephesians 6:10–20; Philippians 3:3.)

6. *I believe apart from Christ I can do nothing, so I declare my complete dependence on Him. I choose to abide in Christ in order to bear much fruit and glorify my Father. I announce to Satan that Jesus is my Lord. I reject any and all counterfeit gifts or works of Satan in my life.* (See John 15:5,8; 1 Corinthians 12:3.)

7. *I believe the truth will set me free, and Jesus is the truth. If He sets me free, I will be free indeed. I recognize that walking in the light is the only path of true fellowship with God and man. Therefore, I stand against all of Satan's deception by taking every thought captive in obedience to Christ. I declare that the Bible is the only authoritative standard for truth and life.* (See John 8:32,36; 14:6; 2 Corinthians 10:5; 2 Timothy 3:15–17; 1 John 1:3–7.)

8. *I choose to present my body to God as a living and holy sacrifice and the members of my body as instruments of righteousness. I choose to renew my mind by the living Word of God in order that I may prove that the will of God is good, acceptable, and perfect. I put off the old self with its evil practices and put on the new self. I declare myself to be a new creation in Christ.* (See Romans 6:13; 12:1–2; 2 Corinthians 5:17; Colossians 3:9–10.)

9. *By faith, I choose to be filled with the Spirit so I can be guided into all truth. I choose to walk by the Spirit so I will not carry out the desires of the flesh.* (See John 16:13; Galatians 5:16; Ephesians 5:18.)

10. *I renounce all selfish goals and choose the ultimate goal of love. I choose to obey the two greatest commandments: to love the Lord my God with all my heart, soul, mind, and strength and to love my neighbor as myself.* (See Matthew 22:37–39; 1 Timothy 1:5.)

11. *I believe the Lord Jesus has all authority in heaven and on earth, and He is the head over all rule and authority. I am complete in Him. I believe Satan and his demons are subject to me in Christ since I am a member of Christ's body. Therefore, I obey the command to submit to God and resist the devil, and I command Satan in the name of Jesus Christ to leave my presence.* (See Matthew 28:18; Ephesians 1:19–23; Colossians 2:10; James 4:7.)

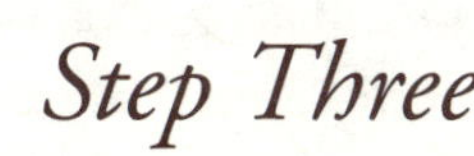

Step Three

BITTERNESS VS. FORGIVENESS

We are called to be merciful just as our Heavenly Father is merciful (Luke 6:36) and forgive others as we have been forgiven (Ephesians 4:31–32). Doing so sets us free from our past and doesn't allow Satan to take advantage of us (2 Corinthians 2:10–11). Ask God to bring to your mind the people you need to forgive by praying the following prayer aloud:

> *Dear heavenly Father, I thank You for the riches of Your kindness, forbearance, and patience toward me, knowing that Your kindness has led me to repentance. I confess that I have not shown that same kindness and patience toward those who have hurt or offended me (Romans 2:4). Instead, I have held on to my anger, bitterness, and resentment toward them. Please bring to my mind all the people I need to forgive in order that I may now do so. In Jesus' name I pray. Amen.*

On a separate sheet of paper, list the names of people who come to your mind. At this point don't question whether you need to forgive them or not. Often we hold things against ourselves as well, punishing ourselves for wrong choices we've made in the past. Write "myself" at the bottom of your list if you need to forgive yourself. Forgiving yourself is accepting the truth that God has already forgiven you in Christ. If God forgives you, you can forgive yourself!

Also write down "thoughts against God" at the bottom of your list. Obviously, God has never done anything wrong so He doesn't need our forgiveness, but we need to let go of our disappointments with our heavenly Father. People often harbor angry thoughts against Him because He did not do what they wanted Him to do. Those feelings of anger or resentment toward God need to be released.

Before you begin working through the process of forgiving those on your list, review what forgiveness is and what it is not. The critical points are highlighted in bold print.

Forgiveness is not forgetting. People who want to forget all that was done to them will find they cannot do it. When God says, *He will remember our sins no more*, He is saying that He will not use the past against us. Forgetting is a long term by-product of forgiveness, but it is never a means toward it. Don't put off forgiving those who have hurt you, hoping the pain will go away. Once you choose to forgive someone, *then* Christ will heal your wounds. We don't heal in order to forgive; we forgive in order to heal.

66 **Forgiveness is a choice, a decision of the will.** Since God requires you to forgive, it is something you can do. Some people hold on to their anger as a means of protecting themselves against further abuse, but all they are doing is hurting themselves. Others want revenge. The Bible teaches, *"Revenge is mine, I will repay," says the Lord* (Romans 12:19). Let God deal with the person. Let him or her off your hook because as long as you refuse to forgive someone, you are still hooked to that person. You are still chained to your past, bound up in your bitterness. By forgiving, you let the other person off your hook, but he or she is not off God's hook. You must trust that God will deal with the person justly and fairly, something you simply cannot do.

But you don't know how much this person hurt me! No other human really knows another person's pain, but Jesus does, and instructs us to forgive others for our sake. Until you let go of your bitterness and hate, the person is still hurting you. Nobody can fix your past, but you can be free from it. What you gain by forgiving is freedom from your past and those who have abused you. Forgiveness is to set a captive free and then realize you were the captive.

Forgiveness is agreeing to live with the consequences of another person's sin. We are all living with the consequences of someone else's sin. The only choice is to do so in the *bondage of bitterness* or in the *freedom of forgiveness.* But where is the justice? The cross makes forgiveness legally and morally right. Jesus died, once for all our sins. We are to forgive as Christ has forgiven us. He did that by taking upon Himself the consequences of our sins. God *made Him who knew no sin to be sin on our behalf, that we might become the righteousness of God in Him* (2 Corinthians 5:21). Do not wait for the other person to ask for your forgiveness. Remember, Jesus did not wait for those who were crucifying Him to apologize before He forgave them. Even while they mocked and jeered at Him, He prayed, *"Father, forgive them; for they do not know what they are doing"* (Luke 23:34).

Forgive from your heart. Allow God to bring to the surface the painful memories and acknowledge how you feel toward those who've hurt you. If your forgiveness doesn't touch the emotional core of your life, it will be incomplete. Too often we're afraid of the pain so we bury our emotions deep down inside us. Let God bring them to the surface so He can begin to heal those damaged emotions.

Forgiveness is choosing not to hold someone's sin against him or her any more. It is common for bitter people to bring up past offenses with those who have hurt them. They want them to feel as bad as they do! But we must let go of the past and choose to reject any thought of revenge. This doesn't mean you continue to put up with the abuse. God does not tolerate sin and neither should you. You will need to set up scriptural boundaries that put a stop to further abuse. Take a stand against sin while continuing to exercise grace and forgiveness toward those who hurt you. If you need help setting scriptural boundaries to protect yourself from further abuse, talk to a trusted friend, counselor, or pastor.

Don't wait until you feel like forgiving. You will never get there. Make the hard choice to forgive even if you don't feel like it. Once you choose to forgive, Satan will lose his hold on you, and God will heal your damaged emotions.

Start with the first person on your list, and make the choice to forgive him or her for every painful memory that comes to your mind. Stay with that individual until you are sure you have dealt with all the remembered pain. Then work your way down the list in the same way.

As you begin forgiving people, God may bring to your mind painful memories you've totally forgotten. Let Him do this even if it hurts. God is surfacing those painful memories so you can face them once for all time and let them go. Don't excuse the offender's behavior, even if it is someone you are really close to.

Don't say, *Lord, please help me to forgive.* He is already helping you and will be with you all the way through the process. Don't say, *Lord, I want to forgive,* because that bypasses the hard choice we have to make. Say, *Lord, I choose to forgive these people and what they did to me.*

For every painful memory that God reveals for each person on your list, pray aloud:

> *Lord Jesus, I choose to forgive* (name the person) *for* (what they did or failed to do), *because it made me feel* (share the painful feelings, e.g., rejected, dirty, worthless, inferior, etc.).

After you have forgiven every person for every painful memory, then pray as follows:

> *Lord Jesus, I choose not to hold on to my resentment. I relinquish my right to seek revenge and ask you to heal my damaged emotions. Thank You for setting me free from the bondage of my bitterness. I now ask You to bless those who have hurt me. In Jesus' name I pray. Amen.*

Before we came to Christ, thoughts were raised up in our minds against a true knowledge of God (2 Corinthians 10:3–5). Even as believers we have harbored resentments toward God and that will hinder our walk with Him. We should have a healthy fear of God (awe of His holiness, power, and presence), but we fear no punishment from Him. Romans 8:15 reads, *For you have not received a spirit of slavery leading to fear again, but you have received a spirit of adoption as sons by which we cry out, "Abba! Father!"*

The following exercise will help renew your mind to a true knowledge of your Heavenly Father. Read out loud through the list starting with the left column and then read the corresponding right column. Begin each one with the statement in bold at the top of that list.

Acknowledging the Truth about Your Father God

I renounce the lie that my Father God is:	**I choose to believe the truth that my God is:**
Distant and disinterested.	Intimate and involved (see Psalm 139:1–18).
Insensitive and uncaring.	Kind and compassionate (see Psalm 103:8–14).
Stern and demanding.	Accepting and filled with joy and love (see Romans 15:7; Zephaniah 3:17).
Passive and cold.	Warm and affectionate (see Isaiah 40:11; Hosea 11:3–4).
Absent or too busy for me.	Always with me and eager to be with me (see Hebrews 13:5; Jeremiah 31:20; Ezekiel 34:11–16).
Never satisfied with what I do; impatient or angry.	Patient and slow to anger (see Exodus 34:6; 2 Peter 3:9).
Mean, cruel or abusive.	Loving, gentle and protective of me (see Jeremiah 31:3; Isaiah 42:3; Psalm 18:2).
Trying to take all the fun out of life.	Trustworthy and wants to give me a full life; His will is good, perfect and acceptable for me (see Lamentations 3:22–23; John 10:10; Romans 12:1–2).
Controlling or manipulative.	Full of grace and mercy, and He gives me freedom to fail (see Hebrews 4:15–16; Luke 15:11–16).
Condemning or unforgiving.	Tenderhearted and forgiving; His heart and arms are always open to me (see Psalm 130:1–4; Luke 15:17–24).
Nit-picking, exacting or perfectionistic.	Committed to my growth and proud of me as His beloved child (see Romans 8:28–29; Hebrews 12:5–11; 2 Corinthians 7:4).

I AM THE APPLE OF HIS EYE!!

Deuteronomy 32:9–10

Step Four

REBELLION VS. SUBMISSION

We live in rebellious times. Many people sit in judgment of those in authority over them, and they submit only when it is convenient, or they do so in the fear of being caught. The Bible instructs us to pray for those in authority over us (1 Timothy 2:1–2), and submit to governing authorities (Romans 13:1–7). Rebelling against God and His established authority leaves us spiritually vulnerable. The only time God permits us to disobey earthly leaders is when they require us to do something morally wrong, or attempt to rule outside the realm of their authority. To have a submissive spirit and servant's heart, pray the following prayer aloud:

> *Dear heavenly Father, You have said that rebellion is as the sin of witchcraft and insubordination is as iniquity and idolatry (1 Samuel 15:23). I know that I have not always been submissive, but instead have rebelled in my heart against You and against those You have placed in authority over me in attitude and in action. Please show me all the ways I have been rebellious. I choose now to adopt a submissive spirit and a servant's heart. In Jesus' name I pray. Amen.*

It is an act of faith to trust God to work in our lives through something less than perfect leaders, but that is what God is asking us to do. Should those in positions of leadership or power abuse their authority and break the laws designed to protect innocent people, you need to seek help from a higher authority. Many states require certain types of abuse to be reported to a governmental agency. If that is your situation, we urge you to get the help you need immediately. Don't, however, assume an authority is violating God's word just because he or she is telling you to do something you don't like. God has set up specific lines of authority to protect us and give order to society. It is the position of authority we respect. Without governing authorities every society would be chaos.

In the list below, allow the Lord to show you any specific ways you have been rebellious and use the prayer following to confess those sins He brings to mind.

- ❑ Civil government (including traffic laws, tax laws, attitude toward government officials) (Romans 13:1–7; 1 Timothy 2:1–4; 1 Peter 2:13–17)
- ❑ Parents, stepparents, or legal guardians (Ephesians 6:1–3)
- ❑ Teachers, coaches, school officials (Romans 13:1–4)
- ❑ Employers (past and present) (1 Peter 2:18–23)
- ❑ Husband (1 Peter 3:1–4) or wife (Ephesians 5:21; 1 Peter 3:7) [Husbands: Ask the Lord if your lack of love for your wife could be fostering a rebellious spirit within her. If so, confess that as a violation of Ephesians 5:22–33.]
- ❑ Church leaders (Hebrews 13:7)
- ❑ God (Daniel 9:5,9)

For each way in which the Spirit of God brings to your mind that you have been rebellious, use the following prayer to specifically confess that sin:

> *Lord Jesus, I confess that I have been rebellious toward* (name or position) *by* (specifically confess what you did or did not do). *Thank You for Your forgiveness. I choose to be submissive and obedient to Your Word. In Jesus' name I pray. Amen.*

Step Five

PRIDE VS. HUMILITY

Pride comes before a fall, but God gives grace to the humble (James 4:6; 1 Peter 5:1–10). Humility is confidence properly placed in God, and we are instructed to, *put no confidence in the flesh* (Philippians 3:3). We are to be, *strong in the Lord and in the strength of His might* (Ephesians 6:10). Proverbs 3:5–7 urges us to trust in the Lord with all our hearts and not lean on our own understanding. Use the following prayer to ask for God's guidance concerning where you may be prideful:

> *Dear heavenly Father, You have said that pride goes before destruction and an arrogant spirit before stumbling. I confess that I have focused on my own needs and desires and not others. I have not always denied myself, picked up my cross daily and followed You. I have relied on my own strength and resources instead of resting in Yours. I have placed my will before Yours and centered my life around myself instead of You. I confess my pride and selfishness and pray that all ground gained in my life by the enemies of the Lord Jesus Christ would be canceled. I choose to rely upon the Holy Spirit's power and guidance so that I will do nothing from selfishness or empty conceit. With humility of mind, I choose to regard others as more important than myself. I acknowledge You as my Lord, and confess that apart from You I can do nothing of lasting significance. Please examine my heart and show me the specific ways I have lived my life in pride. In the gentle and humble name of Jesus I pray. Amen.* (See Proverbs 16:18; Matthew 6:33; 16:24; Romans 12:10; Philippians 2:3.)

Pray through the list below and use the prayer following to confess any sins of pride the Lord brings to mind.

- ❑ Having a stronger desire to do my will than God's will
- ❑ Leaning too much on my own understanding and experience rather than seeking God's guidance through prayer and His Word
- ❑ Relying on my own strengths and resources instead of depending on the power of the Holy Spirit
- ❑ Being more concerned about controlling others than in developing self-control
- ❑ Being too busy doing "important" and selfish things rather than seeking and doing God's will
- ❑ Having a tendency to think that I have no needs
- ❑ Finding it hard to admit when I am wrong
- ❑ Being more concerned about pleasing people than pleasing God
- ❑ Being overly concerned about getting the credit I feel I deserve
- ❑ Thinking I am more humble, spiritual, religious, or devoted than others
- ❑ Being driven to obtain recognition by attaining degrees, titles, and positions
- ❑ Often feeling that my needs are more important than another person's needs
- ❑ Considering myself better than others because of my academic, artistic, athletic abilities, and accomplishments
- ❑ Having feelings of inferiority appearing as false humility
- ❑ Not waiting on God
- ❑ Other ways I have thought more highly of myself than I should

For each of the above areas that has been true in your life, pray aloud:

> *Lord Jesus, I agree I have been proud by* (name what you checked above). *Thank You for Your forgiveness. I choose to humble myself before You and others. I choose to place all my confidence in You and put no confidence in my flesh. In Jesus' name I pray. Amen.*

Step Six

BONDAGE VS. FREEDOM

Many times we feel trapped in a vicious cycle of "sin–confess–sin–confess" that never seems to end. We can become very discouraged and end up just giving up and giving in to the sins of the flesh. In order to experience our freedom we must follow James 4:7: "Submit therefore to God. Resist the devil and he will flee from you." We submit to God by confession of sin and repentance (turning away from sin). We resist the devil by rejecting his lies. We must walk in the truth and put on the full armor of God (see Ephesians 6:10–20).

Sin that has become a habit often may require help from a trusted brother or sister in Christ. James 5:16 says *Confess your sins to one another, and pray for one another, so that you may be healed. The effective prayer of a righteous man can accomplish much.* Sometimes the assurance of 1 John 1:9 is enough: *If we confess our sins, He is faithful and righteous to forgive us our sins and to cleanse us from all unrighteousness.*

Remember, confession is not saying, *I'm sorry.* It is openly admitting, *I did it.* Whether you need help from other people or just the accountability of walking in the light before God, pray the following prayer aloud:

> *Dear Heavenly Father, You have told me to put on the Lord Jesus Christ and make no provision for the flesh in regard to its lust. I confess that I have given in to fleshly lusts that wage war against my soul. I thank You that in Christ my sins are already forgiven, but I have broken Your holy law and I have allowed sin to wage war in my body. I come to You now to confess and renounce these sins of the flesh so that I might be cleansed and set free from the bondage of sin. Please reveal to my mind all the sins of the flesh I have committed and the ways I have grieved the Holy Spirit. In Jesus' holy name, I pray. Amen.* (See Romans 6:12–13; 13:14; 2 Corinthians 4:2; James 4:1; 1 Peter 2:11; 5:8.)

The following list contains many sins of the flesh, but a prayerful examination of Mark 7:20–23, Galatians 5:19–21, Ephesians 4:25–31, and other Scripture passages will help you to be even more thorough. Look over the list below and the Scriptures just listed and ask the Holy Spirit to bring to your mind the ones you need to confess. He may reveal others to you as well. For each one the Lord shows you, pray a prayer of confession from your heart. There is a sample prayer following the list. (*Note:* Sexual sins, eating disorders, substance abuse, abortion, suicidal tendencies, and perfectionism will be dealt with later in this step. Further counseling help may be necessary to find complete healing and freedom in these and other areas.)

- ❑ Stealing
- ❑ Quarreling/fighting
- ❑ Jealousy/envy
- ❑ Complaining/criticism
- ❑ Sarcasm
- ❑ Lustful actions
- ❑ Gossip/slander
- ❑ Swearing
- ❑ Apathy/laziness
- ❑ Lying
- ❑ Hatred
- ❑ Anger
- ❑ Lustful thoughts
- ❑ Drunkenness
- ❑ Cheating
- ❑ Procrastination
- ❑ Greed/materialism
- ❑ Others:

____

____

____

> *Lord Jesus, I confess that I have sinned against You by* (name the sins). *Thank You for Your forgiveness and cleansing. I now turn away from these expressions of sin and turn to You, Lord. Fill me with Your Holy Spirit so that I will not carry out the desires of the flesh. In Jesus' name I pray. Amen.*

Note: If you are struggling with habitual sin, read *Overcoming Addictive Behavior,* (Regal Books, 2003).

Resolving Sexual Sin

It is our responsibility not to allow sin to reign (rule) in our mortal bodies. We must not use our bodies or another person's body as an instrument of unrighteousness (see Romans 6:12–13). Sexual immorality is not only a sin against God, but is sin against your body, the temple of the Holy Spirit (1 Corinthians 6:18–19). To find freedom from sexual bondage, begin by praying the following prayer:

> *Lord Jesus, I have allowed sin to reign in my mortal body. I ask You to bring to my mind every sexual use of my body as an instrument of unrighteousness so that I can renounce these sexual sins and break those sinful bondages. In Jesus' name I pray. Amen.*

As the Lord brings to your mind every immoral sexual use of your body, whether it was done to you (rape, incest, sexual molestation) or willingly by you (pornography, masturbation, sexual immorality), renounce *every* experience as follows:

> *Lord Jesus, I renounce* (name the sexual experience) *with* (name). *I ask You to break that sinful bond with* (name) *spiritually, physically and emotionally.*

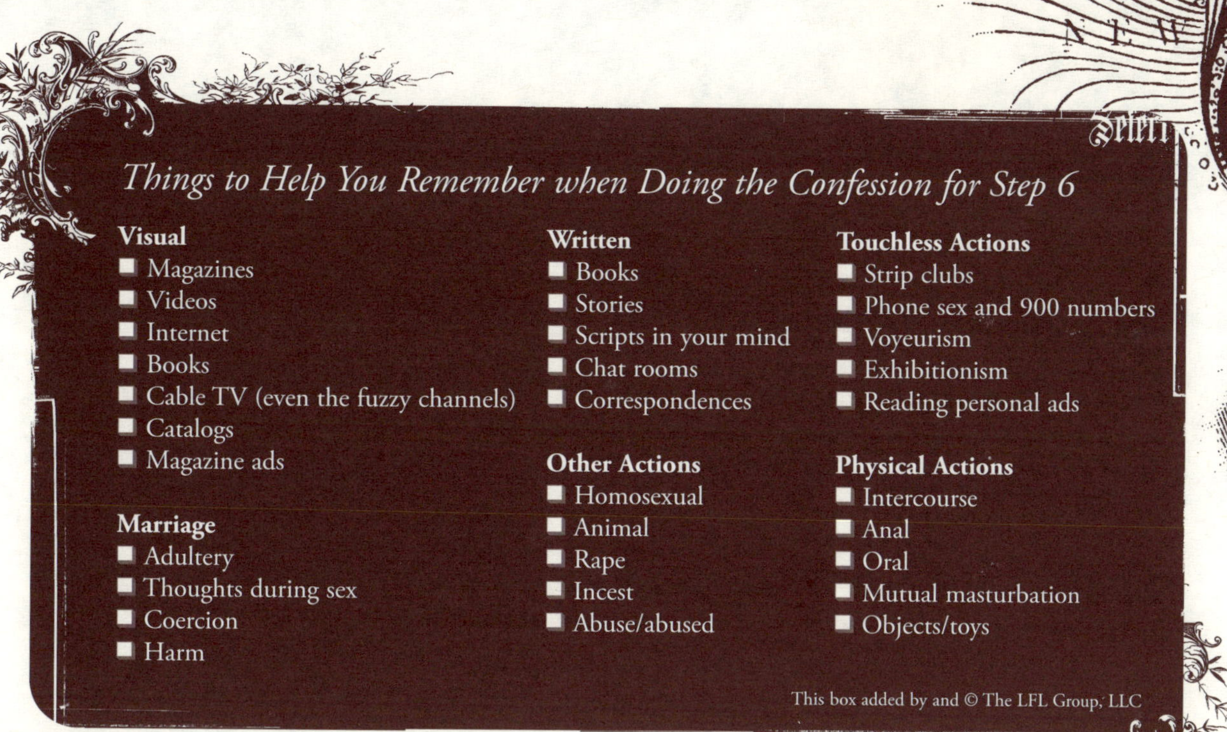

Things to Help You Remember when Doing the Confession for Step 6

Visual
- Magazines
- Videos
- Internet
- Books
- Cable TV (even the fuzzy channels)
- Catalogs
- Magazine ads

Marriage
- Adultery
- Thoughts during sex
- Coercion
- Harm

Written
- Books
- Stories
- Scripts in your mind
- Chat rooms
- Correspondences

Other Actions
- Homosexual
- Animal
- Rape
- Incest
- Abuse/abused

Touchless Actions
- Strip clubs
- Phone sex and 900 numbers
- Voyeurism
- Exhibitionism
- Reading personal ads

Physical Actions
- Intercourse
- Anal
- Oral
- Mutual masturbation
- Objects/toys

This box added by and © The LFL Group, LLC

After you are finished, commit your body to the Lord by praying:

> *Lord Jesus, I renounce all these uses of my body as an instrument of unrighteousness, and I admit to any willful participation. I choose to present my physical body to You as an instrument of righteousness, a living and holy sacrifice, acceptable to You. I choose to reserve the sexual use of my body for marriage only. I reject the devil's lie that my body is not clean or that it is dirty or in any way unacceptable to You as a result of my past sexual experiences. Lord, thank You that You have cleansed and forgiven me and that You love and accept me just the way I am. Therefore, I choose now to accept myself and my body as clean in Your eyes. In Jesus' name I pray. Amen.*

Prayers for Specific Issues

Pornography

> *Lord Jesus, I confess that I have looked at sexually suggestive and pornographic material for the purpose of stimulating myself sexually. I have attempted to satisfy my lustful desires and polluted my body, soul, and spirit. Thank You for cleansing me and for Your forgiveness. I renounce any satanic bonds I have allowed in my life through the unrighteous use of my body and mind. Lord, I commit myself to destroy any objects in my possession that I have used for sexual stimulation, and to turn away from all media that are associated with my sexual sin. I commit myself to the renewing of my mind and to think pure thoughts. Fill me with your Holy Spirit that I may not carry out the desires of the flesh. In Jesus' name I pray. Amen.*

Homosexuality

> *Lord Jesus, I renounce the lie that You have created me or anyone else to be homosexual and I agree that in Your Word You clearly forbid homosexual behavior. I choose to accept myself as a child of God and I thank You that You created me as a man (woman). I renounce all homosexual thoughts, urges, drives, and acts and renounce all ways that Satan has used these things to pervert my relationships. I announce that I am free in Christ to relate to the opposite sex and my own sex in the way that You intended. In Jesus' name I pray. Amen.*

Abortion

Lord Jesus, I confess that I was not a proper guardian and keeper of the life You entrusted to me, and I confess that I have sinned. Thank You that because of Your forgiveness, I can forgive myself. I commit the child to You for all eternity, and believe that he or she is in Your caring hands. In Jesus' name I pray. Amen.

Suicidal Tendencies

Lord Jesus, I renounce all suicidal thoughts and any attempts I've made to take my own life or in any way injure myself. I renounce the lie that life is hopeless and that I can find peace and freedom by taking my own life. Satan is a thief and comes to steal, kill, and destroy. I choose life in Christ who said He came to give me life and give it abundantly. Thank You for Your forgiveness that allows me to forgive myself. I choose to believe that there is always hope in Christ and that my heavenly Father loves me. In Jesus' name, I pray. Amen.

Drivenness and Perfectionism

Lord Jesus, I renounce the lie that my sense of worth is dependent upon my ability to perform. I announce the truth that my identity and sense of worth is found in who I am as Your child. I renounce seeking the approval and acceptance of other people, and I choose to believe that I am already approved and accepted in Christ, because of His death and resurrection for me. I choose to believe the truth that I have been saved, not by deeds done in righteousness, but according to Your mercy. I choose to believe that I am no longer under the curse of the law, because Christ became a curse for me. I receive the free gift of life in Christ and choose to abide in Him. I renounce striving for perfection by living under the law. By Your grace, Heavenly Father, I choose from this day forward to walk by faith in the power of Your Holy Spirit according to what You have said is true. In Jesus' name I pray. Amen.

Eating Disorders or Self-Mutilation

Lord Jesus, I renounce the lie that my value as a person is dependent upon my appearance or performance. I renounce cutting or abusing myself, vomiting, using laxatives or starving myself as a means of being in control, altering my appearance, or trying to cleanse myself of evil. I announce that only the blood of the Lord Jesus Christ cleanses me from sin. I realize I have been bought with a price and my body, the temple of the Holy Spirit, belongs to God. Therefore, I choose to glorify God in my body. I renounce the lie that I am evil or that any part of my body is evil. Thank You that You accept me just the way I am in Christ. In Jesus' name I pray. Amen.

Substance Abuse

Lord Jesus, I confess that I have misused substances (alcohol, tobacco, food, prescription or street drugs) for the purpose of pleasure, to escape reality, or to cope with difficult problems. I confess that I have abused my body and programmed my mind in harmful ways. I have quenched the Holy Spirit as well. Thank You for Your forgiveness. I renounce any satanic connection or influence in my life through my misuse of food or chemicals. I cast my anxieties onto Christ who loves me. I commit myself to yield no longer to substance abuse, but instead I choose to allow the Holy Spirit to direct and empower me. In Jesus' name I pray. Amen.

Overcoming Fear

Fear is a God given natural response when our physical or psychological safety is threatened. Courage is not the absence of fear but living by faith and doing what is right in the face of illegitimate fear objects. The fear of God is the beginning of wisdom and the only fear that can overcome all other fears. Irrational fears compel us to live irresponsible lives, or prevent us from doing that which is responsible and from being a good witness. Behind every irrational fear is a lie, which must be identified. Allow the Lord to surface any controlling fears in your life and any root lies by praying the following prayer:

> *Dear heavenly Father, I confess that I have allowed fear to control me and that lack of faith is sin. Thank You for Your forgiveness. I recognize that You have not given me a spirit of fear, but of power, love and discipline (2 Timothy 1:7). I renounce any spirit of fear operating in my life and ask You to reveal any and all controlling fears in my life and the lies behind them. I desire to live by faith in You and in the power of the Holy Spirit. In Jesus' name I pray. Amen.*

- ❑ Fear of death
- ❑ Fear of never loving or being loved
- ❑ Fear of Satan
- ❑ Fear of embarrassment
- ❑ Fear of failure
- ❑ Fear of being victimized
- ❑ Fear of rejection by people
- ❑ Fear of marriage
- ❑ Fear of disapproval
- ❑ Fear of divorce
- ❑ Fear of becoming/being homosexual
- ❑ Fear of going crazy
- ❑ Fear of financial problems
- ❑ Fear of pain/illness
- ❑ Fear of never getting married
- ❑ Fear of the future
- ❑ Fear of the death of a loved one
- ❑ Fear of confrontation
- ❑ Fear of being a hopeless case
- ❑ Fear of specific individuals; list them:

____

____

____

- ❑ Fear of losing my salvation
- ❑ Fear of not being loved by God
- ❑ Fear of having committed the unpardonable sin
- ❑ Other specific fears that come to mind now:

____

____

____

Analyze Your Fear

When did you first experience the fear, and what events preceded the first experience? What lies have you been believing that is the basis for the fear? How has the fear kept you from living a responsible life or compromised your witness? Confess any active or passive way that you have allowed fear to control you. Work out a plan of responsible behavior, and determine in advance what your response will be to any fear object. Commit yourself to follow through with your plan. If you do the thing you fear the most; the death of fear is certain.

> *Lord Jesus, I renounce the fear of* (name the fear and associated lies) *because God has not given me a spirit of fear. I choose to live by faith in the You, and acknowledge You as the only legitimate fear object in my life. In Jesus' name I pray. Amen.*

Note: For additional help read *Freedom From Fear,* (Harvest House Publishers, 1999).

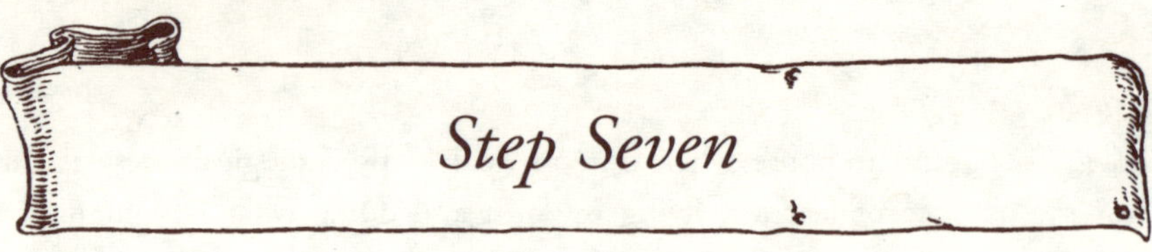

Step Seven

CURSES VS. BLESSINGS

Scripture declares that the iniquities of one generation can be visited on to the third and fourth generations, but God's blessings will be poured out on thousands of generations of those who love and obey Him (Exodus 20:4–6). The iniquities of one generation can adversely affect future ones unless those sins are renounced, and your new spiritual heritage in Christ is claimed. This cycle of abuse and all negative influences can be stopped through genuine repentance. Jesus died for our sins, but that is only appropriated when you choose to believe Him and experienced when you repent. You are not guilty of your ancestor's sins, but because of their sins you were affected by their influence. Jesus said that after we have been fully trained we will be like our teachers (Luke 6:40), and Peter wrote that you were redeemed from your futile way of life inherited from your forefathers (1 Peter 1:18). Ask the Lord to reveal your ancestral sins and then renounce them as follows:

> *Dear heavenly Father, please reveal to my mind all the sins of my ancestors that have been passed down through family lines. Since I am a new creation in Christ, I want to experience my freedom from those influences and walk in my new identity as a child of God. In Jesus' name I pray. Amen.*
>
> *Lord, I renounce* (confess all the family sins that God brings to your mind).

Satan and people may curse us, but it will not have any affect on us unless we believe it. We cannot passively take our place in Christ, we must actively and intentionally choose to submit to God, resist the devil and then he will flee from us. Complete this final step with the following declaration and prayer:

Declaration

I here and now reject and disown all the sins of my ancestors. As one who has been delivered from the domain of darkness and transferred into the kingdom of God's Son, I declare myself to be free from those harmful influences. I am no longer "in Adam." I am now alive "in Christ." Therefore I am the recipient of the blessings of God upon my life as I choose to love and obey Him. As one who has been crucified and raised with Christ and who sits with Him in heavenly places, I renounce any and all satanic attacks and assignments directed against me and my ministry. Every curse placed on me was broken when Christ became a curse for me by dying on the cross (Galatians 3:13). I reject any and every way in which Satan may claim ownership of me. I belong to the Lord Jesus Christ who purchased me with His own precious blood. I declare myself to be fully and eternally signed over and committed to the Lord Jesus Christ. Therefore, having submitted to God and by His authority, I now resist the devil, and I command every spiritual enemy of the Lord Jesus Christ to leave my presence. I put on the armor of God and I stand against Satan's temptations, accusations, and deceptions. From this day forward I will seek to do only the will of my heavenly Father.

Prayer

Dear heavenly Father, I come to You as Your child, bought out of slavery to sin by the blood of the Lord Jesus Christ. You are the Lord of the universe and the Lord of my life. I submit my body to You as a living and holy sacrifice. May You be glorified through my life and body. I now ask You to fill me with Your Holy Spirit. I commit myself to the renewing of my mind in order that I may prove that Your will is good, acceptable, and perfect for me. I desire nothing more than to be like You. I pray, believe, and do all this in the wonderful name of Jesus, my Lord and Savior. Amen.

MAINTAINING YOUR FREEDOM

It is exciting to experience your freedom in Christ, but what you have gained must be maintained. You have won an important battle, but the war goes on. To maintain your freedom in Christ and grow in the grace of God, you must continue renewing your mind to the truth of God's word. If you become aware of lies that you have believed, renounce them and choose the truth. If more painful memories surface, then forgive those who hurt you and renounce any sinful part you played. Many people choose to go through the "Steps to Freedom in Christ" again on their own to make sure they have dealt with all their issues. Often times new issues will surface. The process can assist you in a regular "house cleaning."

It is not uncommon after going though the Steps for people to have thoughts like: *Nothing really changed. You're the same person you always were. It didn't work*. In most cases you should just ignore it. We are not called to dispel the darkness, we are called to turn on the light. You don't get rid of negative thoughts by rebuking every one, you get rid of them by repenting and choosing the truth.

I encourage you to read *Victory Over the Darkness* and *The Bondage Breaker* if you haven't already done so in preparation for going through the Steps. The 21-day devotional, *Walking in Freedom,* was written for those who have gone through the Steps. To continue growing in the grace of God I suggest the following:

1. Get rid of or destroy any cult or occult objects in your home (see Acts 19:18–20).
2. Get involved in a small group ministry where you can be a real person, and be part of a church where God's truth is taught with kindness and grace.
3. Read and meditate on the truth of God's Word each day.
4. Don't let your mind be passive, especially concerning what you watch and listen to (music, TV, etc.). Actively take every thought captive to the obedience of Christ.
5. Learn to pray by the Spirit (see *Praying By the Power of the Spirit,* Regal Books, 2003).
6. Remember, you are responsible for your mental, spiritual, and physical health (for the later see *The Biblical Guide to Alternative Medicine,* Regal Books, 2003).
7. Work through the *Freedom in Christ Bible* (Zondervan), which is a discipleship study Bible that takes you through the sanctifying process five days a week for a year.

Daily Prayer and Declaration

Dear heavenly Father, I praise You and honor You as my Lord and Savior. You are in control of all things. I thank You that You are always with me and will never leave me nor forsake me. You are the only all-powerful and only wise God. You are kind and loving in all Your ways. I love You and thank You that I am united with Christ and spiritually alive in Him. I choose not to love the world or the things in the world, and I crucify the flesh and all its passions.

Thank You for the life I now have in Christ. I ask You to fill me with the Holy Spirit so I can be guided by You and not carry out the desires of the flesh. I declare my total dependence upon You and I take my stand against Satan and all his lying ways. I choose to believe the truth of God's Word despite what my feelings may say. I refuse to be discouraged; You are the God of all hope. Nothing is too difficult for You. I am confident that You will supply all my needs as I seek to live according to Your Word. I thank You that I can be content and live a responsible life through Christ who strengthens me.

I now take my stand against Satan and command him and all his evil spirits to depart from me. I choose to put on the full armor of God so I may be able to stand firm against all the devil's schemes. I submit my body as a living and holy sacrifice to You, and I choose to renew my mind by Your living Word. By so doing I will be able to prove that Your will is good, acceptable, and perfect for me. In the name of my Lord and Savior, Jesus Christ I pray. Amen.

Bedtime Prayer

Thank You, Lord, that You have brought me into Your family and have blessed me with every spiritual blessing in the heavenly places in Christ Jesus. Thank You for this time of renewal and refreshment through sleep. I accept it as one of Your blessings for Your children and I trust You to guard my mind and my body during my sleep.

As I have thought about You and Your truth during the day, I choose to let those good thoughts continue in my mind while I am asleep. I commit myself to You for Your protection against every attempt of Satan and his demons to attack me during sleep. Guard my mind from nightmares. I renounce all fear and cast every anxiety upon You, Lord. I commit myself to You as my rock, my fortress, and my strong tower. May Your peace be upon this place of rest. In the strong name of the Lord Jesus Christ I pray. Amen.

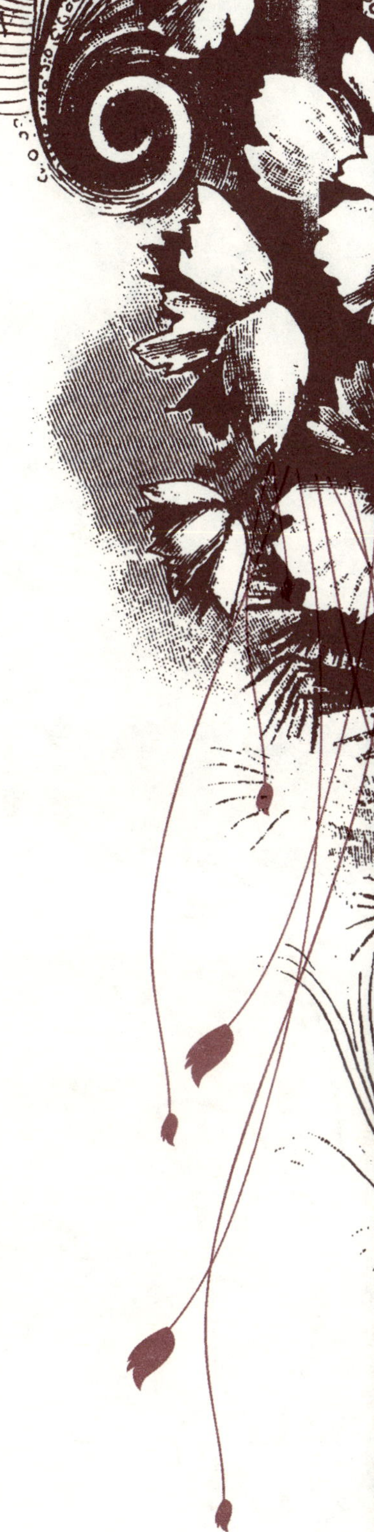

Prayer for Spiritual Cleansing of Home, Apartment, or Room

After removing and destroying all objects of false worship, pray this prayer aloud in every room:

> *Heavenly Father, I acknowledge that You are the Lord of heaven and earth. In Your sovereign power and love, You have entrusted me with many things. Thank You for this place to live. I claim my home as a place of spiritual safety for me and my family and ask for Your protection from all the attacks of the enemy. As a child of God, raised up and seated with Christ in the heavenly places, I command every evil spirit claiming ground in this place, based on the activities of past or present occupants, including me and my family, to leave and never return. I renounce all demonic assignments directed against this place. I ask You, Heavenly Father, to post Your holy angels around this place to guard it from any and all attempts of the enemy to enter and disturb Your purposes for me and my family. I thank You, Lord, for doing this in the name of the Lord Jesus Christ. Amen.*

Prayer for Living in a Non-Christian Environment

After removing and destroying all objects of false worship from your possession, pray this aloud in the place where you live:

> *Thank You, heavenly Father, for a place to live and to be renewed by sleep. I ask You to set aside my room (or portion of this room) as a place of spiritual safety for me. I renounce any allegiance given to false gods or spirits by other occupants. I renounce any claim to this room (space) by Satan based on the activities of past or present occupants, including me. On the basis of my position as a child of God and joint-heir with Christ, who has all authority in heaven and on earth, I command all evil spirits to leave this place and never return. I ask You, heavenly Father, to station Your holy angels to protect me while I live here. In Jesus' mighty name I pray. Amen.*

Paul prays in Ephesians 1:18, *I pray the eyes of your heart may be enlightened, so that you will know what is the hope of His calling, what are the riches of the glory of His inheritance in the saints, and what is the surpassing greatness of His power toward us who believe.* Beloved, you are a child of God (1 John 3:1–3), and *My God will supply all your needs according to His riches in glory in Christ Jesus* (Philippians 4:19). The critical needs are the being needs such as eternal or spiritual life, which He has given you, and an identity, which you have "in Christ." In addition, Jesus has met your needs for *acceptance, security,* and *significance.* Memorize and meditate on the following truths daily from the devotional, *Who I Am in Christ* (Regal Books). Read the entire list aloud, morning and evening, for the next few weeks. Think about what you are reading and let the truth of who you are in Christ renew your mind. This is your inheritance in Christ.

In Christ

I renounce the lie that I am rejected, unloved, or shameful. In Christ I am accepted.
God says:

- *I am God's child* (John 1:12)
- *I am Christ's friend* (John 15:15)
- *I have been justified* (Romans 5:1)
- *I am united with the Lord and I am one spirit with Him* (1 Corinthians 6:17)
- *I have been bought with a price: I belong to God* (1 Corinthians 6:19–20)
- *I am a member of Christ's body* (1 Corinthians 12:27)
- *I am a saint, a holy one* (Ephesians 1:1)
- *I have been adopted as God's child* (Ephesians 1:5)
- *I have direct access to God through the Holy Spirit* (Ephesians 2:18)
- *I have been redeemed and forgiven of all my sins* (Colossians 1:14)
- *I am complete in Christ* (Colossians 2:10)

I renounce the lie that I am guilty, unprotected, alone, or abandoned. In Christ I am secure.
God says:

- *I am free from condemnation* (Romans 8:1–2)
- *I am assured that all things work together for good* (Romans 8:28)
- *I am free from any condemning charges against me* (Romans 8:31–34)
- *I cannot be separated from the love of God* (Romans 8:35–39)
- *I have been established, anointed, and sealed by God* (2 Corinthians 1:21–22)
- *I am confident that the good work God has begun in me will be perfected* (Philippians 1:6)
- *I am a citizen of heaven* (Philippians 3:20)
- *I am hidden with Christ in God* (Colossians 3:3)
- *I have not been given a spirit of fear, but of power, love, and discipline* (2 Timothy 1:7)
- *I can find grace and mercy to help in time of need* (Hebrews 4:16)
- *I am born of God and the evil one cannot touch me* (1 John 5:18)

I renounce the lie that I am worthless, inadequate, helpless, or hopeless. In Christ I am significant.
God says:

- *I am the salt of the earth and the light of the world* (Matthew 5:13–14)
- *I am a branch of the true vine, Jesus, a channel of His life* (John 15:1,5)
- *I have been chosen and appointed by God to bear fruit* (John 15:16)
- *I am a personal, Spirit-empowered witness of Christ's* (Acts 1:8)
- *I am a temple of God* (1 Corinthians 3:16)
- *I am a minister of reconciliation for God* (2 Corinthians 5:17–21)
- *I am God's coworker* (2 Corinthians 6:1)
- *I am seated with Christ in the heavenly realm* (Ephesians 2:6)
- *I am God's workmanship, created for good works* (Ephesians 2:10)
- *I may approach God with freedom and confidence* (Ephesians 3:12)
- *I can do all things through Christ who strengthens me!* (Philippians 4:13)

I am not the great "I Am," but by the grace of God I am what I am.
(See Exodus 3:14; John 8:24, 28, 58; 1 Corinthians 15:10.)

BONUS INFORMATION

86

The Anti-White-Knuckle Approach

The approach I keep reading about in dealing with Christians and sexual issues has been what I would call the "white-knuckle approach." This approach says if you try harder and discipline yourself more that will give you victory over lustful thoughts and actions. Most of us have tried this approach. The question is, "How has it worked for you?" For me and many people I know, the answer is "Not very well."

Paul says in Colossians 2:20–23 NLT, *You have died with Christ, and he has set you free from the evil powers of this world. So why do you keep on following rules of the world, such as, "Don't handle, don't eat, don't touch." Such rules are mere human teaching about things that are gone as soon as we use them. These rules may seem wise because they require strong devotion, humility, and severe bodily discipline. But they have no effect when it comes to conquering a person's evil thoughts and desires.*

In my mind this is as plain as it gets. I have heard the illustration that lust is like a Sumo wrestler and you should starve it. If you starve it out, it will lose strength, and then you will win the battle. Lust, to me, is more like a grizzly bear; starve it if you want but it just hibernates. When it reappears again it will devour you if you don't know how to kill it. Stop starving it, draw your sword of the Spirit and stab it. Kill it off! Yes, it might be a long bloody battle, but with the sword of God's Spirit it can be killed.

If you don't believe you can be free from lust, you believe a lie. You don't manage sin; you die to it—get free from it! Jesus produces inward change in us, not just the external defenses. *Thank God! Once you were slaves of sin, but now you have obeyed with all your heart the new teaching God has given you. Now you are free from sin, your old master, and you have become slaves to your new master, righteousness* (Romans 6:17–18 NLT).

If we don't learn how to first fight spiritually against lust, we will always be tied to the white-knuckle (try harder) approach, which does not produce freedom.

There is some truth in the white-knuckle approach. There are times when we have to be disciplined, and we have to run from and avoid sexual sin as stated by Paul in 1 Corinthians 6:18. These are defensive moves. But Paul gives us more than defense.

All of us know that we cannot win the game with just defense. We also need an offense. We have to learn how to fight in the spiritual world, using the power that Jesus has and allows us to use. Jesus won the game already. All we have to do is claim the victory. *Since we have been united with him in his death, we will also be raised as he was. Our old sinful selves were crucified with Christ so that sin might lose its power in our lives. We are no longer slaves to sin. For when we died with Christ we were set free from the power of sin* (Romans 6:5–7 NLT).

We represent Jesus in this world, and He has given us freedom from sin. That means freedom from lust. *Sin is no longer your master, for you are no longer subject to the law, which enslaves you to sin. Instead, you are free by God's grace* (Romans 6:14 NLT). Trying harder and developing more discipline does not equal freedom. We must also learn and develop an offensive approach to lust.

In 2 Corinthians 10:3–5 NIV, Paul tells us how we must learn to fight: *For though we live in the world, we do not wage war as the world does. The weapons we fight with are not the weapons of the world. On the contrary, they have divine power to demolish strongholds. We demolish arguments and every pretension that sets itself up against the knowledge of God and we take captive every thought to make it obedient to Christ.*

The battle is in our minds, not in the object we are looking at or thinking about. If we just change what we look at, we miss the point. We must change how we think. We must use spiritual weapons, fight with the Truth, take thoughts captive and make them obedient to Christ—battle offensively for our minds first, and then use the defensive strategies. *If your sinful nature controls your mind, there is death. But if the Holy Spirit controls your mind, there is life and peace* (Romans 8:6 NLT).

Our offensive plan that we learned in Lust Free Living is to FIGHT SPIRITUALLY FIRST. Our offense is to fight with the truth of the Word of God, to renounce lies, accept truth and take every thought captive to Jesus. We should draw our swords, fight in the spiritual realm and submit to the Holy Spirit in us.

We need good offensive and defensive strategies—both are needed. Don't be fooled into thinking that having a defensive plan alone will win this battle. Attack the lies and the evil ones with the power you have under the authority of Jesus.

It is said that, "Lusting isn't Satan tempting us, it's really us giving in to our fleshly desires. We seek pleasure more than we seek a holy life with our Creator." If this is all we believe, we miss the issue again. Lust is both our fleshly desires and Satan using lustful thoughts to tempt us. If we learn to first fight lust spiritually in the battle for our minds, then it is a lot easier to have our fleshly desires submit to Jesus.

Freedom does not come from following the rules, it comes from Jesus as we allow Him to be ruler over everything in us. No matter how many rules we follow, they are just rules which *may seem wise because they require strong devotion, humility, and severe bodily discipline. But they have no effect when it comes to conquering a person's evil thoughts and desires* (Colossians 2:22–23 NLT).

I want everyone to know that you can be free from lust. Purity is a battle that Jesus has already won for our minds. All we have to do is step into His victory and be who we are in Christ. Galatians 5:1 NIV says, *It is for freedom that Christ has set us free. Stand firm, then, and do not let yourselves be burdened again by a yoke of slavery.* In the New Living Translation it is stated like this, *So Christ has really set us free. Now make sure that you stay free, and don't get tied up again in slavery to the law.*

In 2 Corinthians 3:16–18 NLT, Paul says, *But whenever anyone turns to the Lord, then the veil is taken away. Now, the Lord is the Spirit, and wherever the Spirit of the Lord is, he gives freedom. And all of us have had that veil removed so that we can be mirrors that brightly reflect the glory of the Lord. And as the Spirit of the Lord works within us, we become more and more like him and reflect his glory even more.*

Paul says in Romans, *What can we say about such wonderful things as these? If God is for us, who can ever be against us? Since God did not spare even his own Son but gave him up for us all, won't God, who gave us Christ, also give us everything else?*

Who dares accuse us whom God has chosen for his own? Will God? No! He is the one who has given us right standing with himself. Who then will condemn us? Will Christ Jesus? No, for he is the one who died for us and was raised to life for us and is sitting at the place of highest honor next to God, pleading for us.

Can anything ever separate us from Christ's love? Does it mean he no longer loves us if we have trouble or calamity, or are persecuted, or are hungry or cold or in danger or threatened with death? (Even the Scriptures say, "For your sake we are killed every day; we are being slaughtered like sheep.") No, despite all these things, overwhelming victory is ours through Christ, who loved us.

And I am convinced that nothing can ever separate us from his love. Death can't, and life can't. The angels can't, and the demons can't. Our fears for today, our worries about tomorrow, and even the powers of hell can't keep God's love away. Whether we are high above the sky or in the deepest ocean, nothing in all creation will ever be able to separate us from the love of God that is revealed in Christ Jesus our Lord (Romans 8:31–39 NLT).

Enjoy your freedom!

This Is HIS Issue, Not Mine

I often have conversations with women who seem perplexed when I tell them the ministry of LFL is not just for men but women too. When we talk about lust, they usually talk about their boyfriend, fiancé or husband who is struggling with pornography, masturbation or adultery. To consider going through our material for themselves makes no sense because they don't have the same problems as the man in their life. "He needs this, not me, right!?

My husband and I started dating in high school. We still face challenges with lust, but the victory in our lives is huge, and I want to share about our healing process for the sake of encouraging you. We both saw dramatic results when we changed how we look at the core problem—lust.

In our case, when I learned of my husband's struggles with lust, I usually reacted with an outburst followed by shutting down emotionally. Then I quickly shifted into "fix it" mode. I had all these great ideas to help him: plant a beautifully framed picture of myself next to the computer, go to the nearest Christian bookstore to read self-help books and even carefully suggest a few to him. I thought about encouraging him to get an accountability partner, surfing the web for the most efficient content filter or throwing the TV out the window.

As time went by, I did what many of us do who share this struggle. I fearfully asked questions to see if he "did it again" or just manipulated the conversation to see if I could coax an answer out of him. Essentially I wound up feeling powerless, frustrated, defeated, cheated and hopeless. And so did he. We were stuck. Can you relate?

Many of us have been there with the man in our life. The pain is deep and feels earth shaking—sometimes all we can think about is how to help him stop. So we do what women often do—we try to control the problem. What I want to challenge you to do is look at "the problem" differently.

The Christian man in our life is in a spiritual battle. He is under great attack all the time, just as we are. When he faces sexual temptation and sin, it is an attack aimed to defeat both him and us. During these painful times, we have to know who our true enemy is (Ephesians 6:12) and what his goals are. He desires to poison our relationships with shame, hopelessness, defeat, darkness, division, deception and despair. In his crafty attempts to destroy us, one of the best things he can do is attack our boyfriend, fiancé or husband in ways that would undermine the power and strength of his manhood, leadership and childlike faith.

While attacking our man, the enemy is also working hard to thwart our confidence as women—our purpose, desirability, beauty and gentleness. The enemy's goal is to use lust in our man's life to bring defeat to both of us. And what happens then? Division. In the eyes of the evil one, that is the perfect outcome!

When the man you love, believe in and desire is struggling with these things, it's important to remember the main problem is not the pornography, masturbation or whatever the symptoms are. The main problem is ALWAYS the thoughts he is having before, during and after and the lies he is choosing to believe.

As we face the effects of lust, we are not abnormal when we hurt. It is painful, and there is reason to grieve. It hurts to know he was looking at other images besides you. What actually hurts more (the real problem in us) are the thoughts that come into our minds about ourselves: You are not enough; not pretty enough, skinny enough, sexy enough, fun enough, loveable enough, etc. Then we go to him and compound the problem by asking question like, "Am I not attractive or desirable enough to you?" Here's the deal—the actual problem isn't about us, and it isn't even about him. Misunderstanding this only produces more shame and confusion.

As women, the most helpful thing we can do in these times is speak the truth of their identity in Christ as well as our own (as the first chapter of LFL teaches—our identity does not come from what we have done but rather what Jesus has done for us). We must deal with our own emotions in a productive way so we can see the real problem and fight for each other.

As for the lies we are faced with, we have to recognize the truth that we are perfectly adored, beautiful, desired, acceptable and chosen by our first love—our Creator. We have to choose to believe the truth no matter the circumstances around us. So when you discover your man responding to lust, you have one of two choices. You believe the lies coming at you about your worth, beauty and desirability and respond with disgust, shaming comments, defeat, withdrawal and punishment; or you take a moment by yourself with God to submit your thoughts and emotions to Him, renounce the lies in Jesus' name and make the choice to believe the truth about yourself and your man. Then you are better able to see the real problem (the spiritual opposition and lies) and fight against them with him.

My husband and I have had quite the journey together, but when he went through LFL in college, freedom began to be something he understood and fought for. I realized my "great ideas" weren't helping—in fact I was making things more challenging for him and our relationship. I had a lot of pain and confusion of my own to deal with. I went through LFL and the Steps to Freedom and the spiritual battle at hand became glaringly obvious to me. I was able to see the affects of the sin of lust not only in his life, but also in mine.

We still face painful times now and then, and I don't always respond well, nor does he. But here is an example of a really productive process for us: Somehow I will find out he bought into lustful temptation. He will share with me what happened, and I will pause for a moment, hearing all the lies tempting me, yet choosing not to believe them. I pull him into my arms and tell him I love him—that he is perfect to me, and I know who he is, who he belongs to and that this has NOTHING to do with him, but everything to do with who his enemy is. Now it's his choice whether he chooses to believe that or not.

It isn't always so eloquent, but it goes something like that. If he hasn't already, I encourage him to call a friend he is accountable with and talk through the details. If it is true that WHAT he did isn't the problem, then I don't need to concern myself with the details (which in times past I wanted to know, so I could have more control). I know what the problem is—his freedom as God's boy was attacked by our enemy. I want to intercede for him and encourage him. I want him and his accountability/fighting partners to work through the details and the rest of the healing process. I have to trust that. If I take it all into my own hands, I will be a ragged, controlling mess.

Let's get back to us as women. Like our men, we need to learn about the spiritual battle at work against us, so we're free to experience the perfection of sexuality and love. It starts with us reframing how we think about our identity, sexuality and temptations. We need to fight TOGETHER and not be divided by lies and deception. We must intercede for the man in our life, remembering he is God's boy—he is one dangerous man and that's good!

We can be part of our man's road to truth, healing and freedom, or we can be part of the shameful force keeping him feeling defeated and silent. Let's live from our hearts where we actually believe what God says about us. Then we can add HIS strength in us to this battle. It's a fun process, so let's armor up and learn how to fight together! For our struggle is not against flesh and blood (our husbands) but against the rulers, against the authorities, against the powers of this dark world and against the spiritual forces of evil in the heavenly realms (Ephesians 6:12).

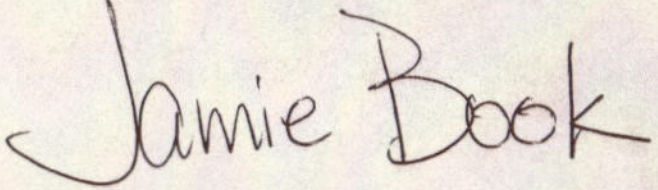

Sexual Addiction: It's Not Getting Better

By Keith Hankinson

A continuum can be used to describe where we stand with certain areas of our lives. For example, with regard to alcohol use, all of us are somewhere on a continuum. We can be a non-user (total abstainer), or a mild user (champagne at a wedding and wine a few times a year on a special occasion), or a social drinker (have alcohol whenever out with friends). At the other end of the continuum, we can be into heavy social use, harmful dependency, or ultimately, chronic addiction.

In the same way, we are all on a continuum with our sexuality. We can be at the low end, which means that we are always in control of our sexual choices (have never made poor sexual choices), and we never abuse our own personal sexuality. I would say that few of us fit onto that part of the continuum. Then it escalates up to the far end of the continuum to chronic sexual addiction, where a person is truly out of control. At the far end of sexual addiction are legal consequences, disease consequences, or tissue damage (in the case of extreme compulsive masturbation). A lot of people can relate to being somewhere on this sexuality continuum. However, if this curriculum has not been helpful and you have not had victory over your problems with sexual lust through this series of teaching and times of prayer, perhaps it's because you're on the sexuality continuum further toward addiction or even in the addiction arena. If this is the case, you need to explore some things more deeply.

Sexual addiction is when we make sexual choices that repeatedly violate our values (God's rules for our life sexually). As Christians, we know that God's precepts are life to us. They are good for us and they enhance our lives. Therefore, obeying God's rules for our sexuality gives us meaningful lives. So, one definition of being sexually compulsive (out of control) or sexually addicted would be that you continue to make bad sexual choices even though they harm you. In other words, there are spiritual, emotional, and legal consequences, and/or you've put your life in danger by putting your body at risk with disease.

No matter how many promises you make to yourself and to God, you seem to break those boundaries and those promises, and you do the very thing you don't want to do. The payoff becomes smaller for the pleasure obtained, but yet you continue to make those sexual choices. After dozens and even hundreds of promises, you still find yourself going back to those same behaviors. These would be signs of sexual addiction.

There is good news for any of you that are feeling out of control sexually and not finding the help you need from this curriculum (teaching). In today's world, we have a lot of resources and it's finally less shaming to ask for help.

Today there are full-time treatment centers for sexually addicted adults and young people. There are also support groups in churches and in the community, Christian therapists specializing in sexual addiction counseling, and accountability mentoring relationships in churches.

The good news is that if a person really desires to get their life under control, to be consistent with God's word and have a lust free life, there are lots of resources available.

The following are signs of sexual addiction developed by Dr. Patrick Carnes. Read them and see if you think you have a sexual addiction problem.

- A pattern of out-of-control behavior.
- Severe consequences due to sexual behavior.
- Inability to stop despite adverse consequences.
- Persistent pursuit of self-destructive or high-risk behavior.
- Ongoing desire or effort to limit sexual behavior.
- Sexual obsession and fantasy as a primary coping strategy.
- Increasing amounts of sexual experiences because the current level of activity is no longer sufficient.
- Severe mood changes around sexual activity.
- Inordinate amounts of time spent in obtaining sex, being sexual or recovering from sexual experience.
- Neglect of important social, occupational or recreational activities because of sexual behavior.[xvi]

If most of these sound like you, please find a professional Christian counselor (preferably one who has worked with sexual addicts).

The following books are recommended to help you.
Freedom from Addiction by Neil T Anderson and Mike & Julia Quarles
A Way of Escape by Neil T. Anderson

If you need crisis mediation or intervention nationwide, call Hankinson Intervention Inc. at 612-382-5051.

Homosexuality: Where to Turn for Help

Many people have had some sort of homosexual experience or tendencies at some point in their lives. I want you to know that this is not uncommon, and you are not alone.

Lustful homosexual thoughts are to be dealt with just like all other lustful thoughts. If you struggle with these thoughts a lot, here are the best resources I have found. There are many organizations that can help you. I will list just two, but you can contact them or visit their Web sites and search for a helping ministry in your area.

Exodus International, North America is a great place to look for help on homosexual issues. You can contact them at:

Exodus International, North America
P.O. Box 77625
Seattle, WA 98177
Phone: 206-784-7799

Their Web address is: **www.ExodusNorthAmerica.org** and make sure to check out the link to "Find a Ministry." Hopefully you can find an organization close to you.

The Portland Fellowship
P.O. Box 9205
Portland, Oregon 97207
E-mail: office@portlandfellowship.com
Phone: 503-235-6364

Their Web site is great and can be found at: **www.PortlandFellowship.com**

They sell an excellent interactive CD titled **The Map**. It's totally worth the price. If you have struggled at all with homosexual thoughts or actions, buy this CD and watch it.

Don't be afraid to contact them and ask for help. Most of the people who staff these organizations are former homosexuals or have dealt with the effects of homosexuality in their lives.

Another great informational resource on the Internet is www.narth.org.

Satan and Our Thoughts

The following is a reading from *Daily In Christ* by Dr. Neil T. & Joanne Anderson.

And take...the sword of the Spirit, which is the word of God (Ephesians 6:17).

The Word of God is the only offensive weapon mentioned in the list of armor. Since Paul used *rhema* instead of logos for "word" in Ephesians 6:17, I believe Paul is referring to the spoken Word of God. We are to defend ourselves against the evil one by speaking aloud God's Word.

Why is it so important to speak God's Word in addition to believing it and thinking it? Because Satan is a created being, and he doesn't perfectly know what you're thinking. By observing you, he can pretty well tell what you are thinking, just as any student of human behavior can. And it isn't difficult for him to know what you're thinking if he put the thought in. But he doesn't know what you're going to do before you do it. He can put thoughts into your mind, and he will know whether you buy his lie by how you behave.

Satan can try to influence you by planting thoughts in your head, but he can't read your thoughts. If you're going to resist Satan, you must do so verbally so he can understand you and be put to flight.

You can communicate with God in your mind and spirit because He knows the thoughts and intents of your heart (Hebrews 4:12). Your unspoken communion with God is your private sanctuary; Satan cannot eavesdrop on you. But by the same token, if you only tell Satan with your thoughts to leave, he won't leave because he is under no obligation to obey your thoughts. You must defeat Satan by speaking out using the all-powerful name of Jesus.

Most direct attacks occur at night or when you are alone. One night I woke up absolutely terrified for no apparent reason, and I knew it was an attack from Satan. Without lifting my head from the pillow, I applied the two-step remedy suggested in James 4:7. In the sanctuary of my heart, I submitted to God. Then I was able to resist Satan with one spoken word—Jesus—and the fear was instantly and totally gone. I went back to sleep in complete peace.

Lord, give me courage to take my stand in this world and defeat Satan by speaking Your Word.[xvii]

Feelings Chart

Satisfied
Refreshed
Completed
Fulfilled
Gratified
Gleeful
Delighted
Peaceful
Tranquil
Calm
Relieved
Comfortable
Contented
Loved
Warm
Wonderful
Friendly
Concerned
Patient
Sick
Curious
Trusted
Bright
Skeptical
Trapped
Cornered
Defeated
Helpless
Inadequate

Lost
Desperate
Hopeless
Invincible
Despondent
Doubtful
Suspicious
Discouraged
Indignant
Irritated
Belligerent
Hostile
Grumpy
Bugged
Aggravated
Annoyed
Irritated
Enraged
Mad
Grouchy
Depressed
Unhappy
Sorry
Pitiful
Dejected
Gloomy
Hurt
Wounded
Ashamed

Crushed
Overwhelmed
Put down
Rejected
Humbled
Disgusted
Cocky
Bold
Confident
Tough
Frightened
Scared
Anxious
Nervous
Jumpy
Jittery
Appalled
Apprehensive
Worried
Restless
Cowardly
Astonished
Startled
Mistrusting
Cautious
Intense
Flighty
Spunky
Brave

Avoiding
Indifferent
Relieved
Humiliated
Warmth toward
Affection for
Tenderness toward
Drawn toward
Friendly toward
Captivated by
Concerned for
Loved by
Longing for
Craving for
Desiring for
Wonder at
Attracted by
Turned away from
Withdrawn from
Rejection of
Distant from
Repelled by
Get away from
Escape from
Evaded by
Startled by
Passion for

Notes

Lesson 1

i Dr. Neil T. Anderson, *Victory Over Darkness* (California: Regal Books—a division of Gospel Light Publications, Ventura, CA 93006), p 43.

ii These questions are taken from a bookmark (Item No. 0002) printed for Freedom In Christ Ministries, La Habra, CA 90631. They adapted it from *Resolving Spiritual Conflicts and Cross-Cultural Ministry* by Dr. Timothy Warner.

iii Dr. Neil T. Anderson, *Victory Over Darkness* (California: Regal Books—a division of Gospel Light Publications, Ventura, CA 93006), p 161.

Lesson 2

iv Miles McPherson, *Sex, Lies and the Truth Video* (Colorado: Focus on the Family, 1993).

v Thomas F. Jones, "Singleness," Discipleship Journal, Issue 64, July/August 1991, pp 35–36.

Lesson 3

vi Josh McDowell, *Maximum Sex* Audio Tape (Texas: Liberation Tapes, 1980).

vii Rev. Ed Silvoso, *Life Encounter Seminar II Workbook* (Harvest Evangelism, Inc. n.d.), p 17.

viii Dr. Neil T. Anderson with Joanne Anderson, *Daily In Christ,* (Oregon: Harvest House Publishers, 2000), March 24 Reading, Copyright © 2000 Used by permission.

ix Rev. Ed Silvoso, *That None Should Perish* (California: Regal Books—a division of Gospel Light Publications, Ventura, CA 93006), p 154.

Lesson 4

x Jim Hancock with Kara Eckmann Powell, *Good Sex* (Michigan: Zondervan—Youth Specialties Books 2001), p 91.

Lesson 5

xi Brennan Manning, *The Ragamuffin Gospel* (Oregon: Multnomah Publishers, Inc. 2000) p 74.

xii Personal interview with Keith Hankinson of Hankinson Intervention, February 4, 2001.

xiii Brennan Manning, *The Ragamuffin Gospel* (Oregon: Multnomah Publishers, Inc. 2000) p 114.

Lesson 7

xiv Dr. Neil T. Anderson, Dave Park and Rich Miller, *The Steps to Freedom In Christ—Youth Edition* (California: Freedom in Christ Ministries), p 12.

Continuing the Fight

xv Dr. Neil T. Anderson, Dave Park and Rich Miller, *The Steps to Freedom In Christ—Youth Edition* (California: Freedom in Christ Ministries), p 12.

Bonus Information:

Sexual Addiction: It's Not Getting Better

xvi Patrick Carnes, Ph.D., *Don't Call it Love* (New York: Bantam Books, 1991) p.11

Satan and Our Thoughts

xvii Dr. Neil T. Anderson with Joanne Anderson, *Daily In Christ* (Oregon: Harvest House Publishers, 2000), November 29 Reading, Copyright © 2000 Used by permission.

***The Steps to Freedom in Christ* section of this book,** by Neil T. Anderson. Copyright © 2005 All rights reserved. No portion of this section may be reproduced, stored in a retrieval system, or transmitted in any form or by any means—electronic, mechanical, photocopy, recording or any other—except for brief quotations in printed reviews, without prior permission from Neil T. Anderson.

All Scripture quotations, unless otherwise indicated, are taken from the Holy Bible, New International Version, NIV. Copyright 1973, 1978, 1984 by International Bible Society. Used by permission of Zondervan Publishing House. All Rights Reserved.